DORDOGN

Arthur Eperon is one of the [...] best-known travel writers in Europe. Since leaving the RAF in 1945 he has worked as a journalist in various capacities, often involving travel. He has concentrated on travel writing for the past twenty-five years and contributed to many publications including *The Times*, *Daily Telegraph* and *New York Times*, and was Travel Editor of the *Sunday Times* magazine. He has also appeared on radio and television and for five years was closely involved in Thames Television's programme *Wish You Were Here*. He has been wine writer to the RAC publications and a number of magazines.

He has an intimate and extensive knowledge of France and its food and wine as a result of innumerable visits there over the last forty years. In 1974 he won the *Prix des Provinces de France*, the annual French award for travel writing. The French Government has now awarded him the *Médaille du Mérite Touristique*. His *Travellers' France* topped the paperback bestseller list for eleven weeks.

**EPERON'S
FRENCH
REGIONAL
GUIDES**

DORDOGNE &
CORRÈZE

ARTHUR EPERON

PAN BOOKS
LONDON, SYDNEY AND AUCKLAND

First published 1991 by Pan Books Ltd,
Cavaye Place, London SW10 9PG

1 3 5 7 9 8 6 4 2

© Arthur Eperon 1991
Illustrations © Mary Fraser 1991
Maps © Ken Smith 1991

ISBN 0 330 31738 5

Designed by Peter Ward
Photoset by Parker Typesetting Service, Leicester
Printed in England by Clays Ltd, St Ives plc

CONTENTS

1 *Departments of France*

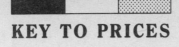

KEY TO PRICES

ROOMS		MEALS	
	A = Under 100F		A = Under 75F
	B = 100–150F		B = 75–90F
	C = 150–200F		C = 90–125F
	D = 200–250F		D = 125–150F
	E = 250–350F		E = 150–175F
	F = 350–450F		F = 175–225F
	G = over 450F		G = over 225F

Room prices per night for double room without breakfast.
Meal prices include tax and service.

INTRODUCTION

My love affair with the Dordogne began in 1952, when most Britons had never heard of it and most Frenchmen would not have dreamed of going there. Even the few young people who still lived there were hurrying away to the cities to enjoy the prosperity of France's post-war industrial boom, as any goods made in the factories were snapped up and almost anyone could get a well-paid job. Well-paid, anyway, by the standards of youngsters helping their fathers to scratch a living on a tiny farm.

In the 1930s Henry Miller called the Dordogne 'The nearest thing to Paradise this side of the Greek Isles'. When my wife and I found it, it was as lush and beautiful as he had described it. The rivers and streams, rich in trout, brushed banks of pleasant, shady trees. Hordes of ducks and geese waddled hurriedly across hillsides, then changed direction suddenly, as if they had spotted something worth eating. Ancient castles and medieval fortified villages called *bastides* beckoned from hilltops. Old inns offered huge meals of thick country soups, rich pâtés, *confits* of duck and goose in flavoursome Perigordian sauce, which they served with sliced potatoes baked in goose fat, hunks of cheese and fruit tart with litres of wine at giveaway prices. Horses and oxen pulled ploughs and carts. There were very few tractors and the few there were were antiquated and falling apart. None of the shiny, cheap, little Ferguson and Ford post-war tractors which were bringing an agricultural revolution to most of West Europe had reached the Dordogne and no one had seen a combine harvester.

It was all beautifully calm, totally peaceful, and sad. The countryside was in decay. Farms and cottages were derelict. The women labouring in the fields looked old and numbed, the men as if they had stopped hoping. Even the old walnut trees, planted in years past by every farmer when he married and took over a farm so that his grandchildren would not starve, looked abandoned and forgotten.

I was offered an eight-room stone farmhouse with a small orchard and large paddock for £650, cottages with slightly leaky roofs, broken doors and outside privies for around £150.

Four of us agreed not to write about the Dordogne. It was not ready for tourists. Then a woman travel-writer for one of the weighty Sunday newspapers was very ill. Afterwards she needed somewhere peaceful with good food to recover. One of us, a PR with British European Airways, sent her to Ogée Delbos, the splendid Bordelais chef who ran the comfortable Hotel Madelaine at Sarlat. Even Sarlat was a decaying hide-out, known only to connoisseurs of France.

The lady travel-writer promised not to write about the area. She wrote six articles in a few weeks. One of London's more exclusive estate agents moved in, offering cottages 'ripe for development'. That was the first of many lessons that taught me that nothing is exclusive in travel and that you cannot hide areas, villages, little hotels or restaurants, however remote, from travellers and tourists.

Anyway, the French Government was looking for ways of rehabilitating its deserted country areas. The Agricultural Ministry gave big subsidies and easy loans for the building or conversion of *gîtes* to help small farmers to stay in business and they deliberately made the Dordogne into something of a tourist area, offering subsidies to Parisians and Bordelais to convert semi-derelict cottages into second holiday homes. The wartime Resistance leader of the Dordogne and Lot, the flamboyant novelist André Malraux who had become de Gaulle's Minister of Culture, introduced a law for the restoration and protection of old buildings and sectors of towns, and began with Sarlat.

Now Sarlat, Périgueux and Brantôme can be very crowded in midsummer. But the Dordogne has no large hotels, or apartment blocks. Visitors stay in small hotels, some made from old manor houses or '*gentilhommeries*'; in modernized cottages or farmhouses which owners use only part of the year and let the rest of it; on campsites; or in *gîtes*, which can mean anything from an apartment in a château or a new bungalow to a restored cottage or farmhouse, or a converted barn.

Towns may be busy but the countryside is never crowded. There are still so few people living there that in whole areas you can easily lose yourself – either by design or by accident – among the little lanes that join secretive hamlets and lone farms among rich meadows, wooded hillsides, walnut plantations and vineyards. Recently, we got lost for two hours and saw no one but people working away in the distance. There was no answer from any of the cottages at which we knocked – just a beagle in the centre of a tiny hamlet's only street, who complained loudly at our intrusion on his peace. Everyone was away in the fields. When, finally, we found ourselves, we were just 6km from the busy N89.

Forêt de Landais and Forêt de la Double on the western edge of the Dordogne hardly get a mention, even in the *Michelin Green Guide*, and are almost as little known to the French as to the British. There are very few buildings in parts of the Double Forest – the wildest part of the Dordogne. It stretches west from Périgueux to the Gironde border. It was once a huge forest of oaks, chestnuts and pines with thick undergrowth, its few clearings made by charcoal burners or by squatters who scratched a living from wood and pigs. Then Napoleon felled a number of trees to build ships and more were felled later for railway sleepers. Water turned the clay soil to marshland and malaria took over. The few who had scraped a living there either died or left.

Then Napoleon III, who had made major improvements and additions to the forestation in Les Landes and the Sologne in the Loire, financed a land reclamation scheme, which was overseen by Trappist monks. They drained marshes, planted vines and raised cattle. Today, malaria has gone, but sixty per cent of it is woodland again and visitors seldom come here.

Few people realize how far west the Dordogne spreads. The British, in particular, loosely use the name Dordogne to cover anywhere near the Dordogne river and for places such as St Céré in Lot and Brive in Corrèze. In fact, it *is* rather confusing that Souillac and Rocamadour are just outside the Dordogne in the Lot department. You can read about this area in my book *Lot (Quercy)* (Pan, £5.99) in this series. But I have included Rocamadour briefly in this book, too (*see* Sites, page 64), because it is officially the second most important tourist site in France and almost every visitor to the Dordogne goes to see it.

The department of the Dordogne is the third largest in France. It was created in 1790 and covers almost the same area as the old Périgord province. There was an argument about its name, so it was called after the river. Even today, older people still call it 'Périgord' and refer to themselves as 'Périgourdins'.

As with much of France, rivers have made the landscape and the history of Dordogne. The many streams and tributaries make a network feeding the Dordogne river, and for centuries the rivers were the main means of transport for goods, livestock and sometimes people. The most important tributaries are the Dronne, Isle, Auvézère and Vézère. With the Dordogne they have brought down rich soil which has settled between limestone and rocks.

The rivers cut caves below ground and these were home to prehistoric man. Discoveries here in the last century have taught us more about our earliest ancestors than any other discoveries elsewhere in the world. Archaeological remains have been found from Neanderthal man who lived about 150,000 years ago, to *Homo sapiens*, who wandered the earth 40,000 years ago.

The Dordogne river is 500km long, one of the longest in France. Its source is 1886 metres up in the Massif Central at the icy peak of Puy de Sancy. It produces nearly one fifth of France's electricity from five hydro-electric dams which control its flow for 120km in the higher reaches in Corrèze.

When the river was used for transport, Souillac, just over the border in Lot, was the main trading port. Staves for barrels and vine stakes were brought down river to Souillac from the Auvergne mountains, then moved on to the *gabares* (poled, flat-bottomed boats with sails) which also took wine and corn. The bigger ones sometimes took cattle, sheep and passengers. There were several dangerous stretches, with choppy, fast-moving waters. The worst stretch, where many lives were lost, was downstream from Mauzac at Sault de Gratusse, a 100-metre stretch of rapids. Boatmen needed a pilot there until it was bypassed by the Lalinde canal in the 1840s. From Lalinde, the journey to Libourne was faster. The big boats from Bergerac came up as far as Lalinde and down to Libourne, shipping mostly wine. The boats used Libourne to try to avoid the taxes put on wines at Bordeaux, which was dominating the wine export market.

The journey of about 200km from Souillac to Libourne took about three days. The small *gabares* were then broken up and sold for their timber and the boatmen would buy a mule, return on it and sell it to a farmer. The big boats had a dreadful journey back against the current, usually carrying salt, a vital and heavily taxed commodity in those days. (Salting meat and vegetables was the only way of keeping them for the winter.) There was only one month in the year when the Dordogne was suitable for taking boats back upstream. At other times it was too low or too fast and dangerous. Local farmers called '*bouviers-haleurs*' provided teams of oxen, each of which could tow the boat for up to 6km. The cliffs, past which the Dordogne flows in many places, were the biggest problem. There the towpath moved across river and poling the boats across the current was difficult and dangerous.

The boats brought a sort of prosperity to riverside villages. Farmers, carpenters, sawyers, blacksmiths and innkeepers all relied on the boats for a large part of their income. This situation lasted until the Coutras- and Brive-to-Périgueux railways

opened in 1857–60. Soon poverty struck most of the villages. Now, however, the Dordogne provides power and watersports. Many riverside villages have beaches, canoes and coarse fishing. Some have campsites. There are summer boat trips and water fêtes.

A few years ago I took a *gabare* down the Dordogne – a modern version, made of a light alloy, and propelled by a pole with an auxiliary engine. The pole was used mostly for steering. The skipper was a sailing instructor from Brittany, but the river was low because of a dry summer and the dams higher up, and he could not prevent us from sticking on mid-river gravel banks where the water was too shallow to use the engine. There were six of us aboard, including a large, tough Paris *flic* who looked and sounded every inch a French copper, but somehow I was always landed with the job of jumping into the icy water and shaking the boat free. '*Tremblant*', they called it. They all encouraged me vocally but none got out of the boat to lighten it. The privilege of belonging to a maritime nation, I suppose.

But it was a superb trip, especially when we stopped at a riverside inn or beneath the cliff and walls of an ancient château, with its overgrown boatmen's steps to the castle ramparts. We saw the great châteaux at Beynac, Montfort and Castelnaud, and the magnificent medieval village of Domme, which sits on a craggy rock overlooking the Dordogne valley. The French people with us made constant jibes about nice convenient chutes for pouring hot '*confiture*' (jam – i.e. boiling oil) on to attacking Englishmen, so at Château de Fénelon, when they were tutting sadly over a picture of Fénelon, the writer, priest and politician, being carried wounded off the battlefield after fighting the Duke of Marlborough at Malplaquet, I said quietly, 'That's what happens to people who tangle with the Churchill family.'

The scenery was also a delight, particularly when sweeping round the Cingles at Montfort and Trémolat, where the Dordogne river turns in almost a complete circle. The variety in the landscape and agriculture in the Dordogne makes driving around it a constant pleasure. With its many tranquil hills and woods it is still the most beautiful area of France for pure relaxation. And the many châteaux are fascinating, for, unlike the beautiful Loire châteaux, they were built for war.

Department boundaries in France are inconvenient and often illogical, even by historic standards and certainly in relation to the road system. The Dordogne–Lot boundary just west of Souillac is strange; so is the Dordogne–Corrèze boundary, which cuts across the N89 Périgueux to Brive road, putting Brive in Corrèze, then continues down the N20 to the Lot border. That is why I have included Corrèze in this book, it is usually lumped with Haute-Vienne and Creuse. The Dordogne river runs south-west right through Corrèze before crossing the Lot border just before the river Cère joins it.

Apart from the commercial town of Brive and the industrial town of Tulle, Corrèze is even less discovered than the remote corners of Dordogne and Lot. It is a land of a million tiny lanes with superb trees of many varieties, and, in the east, of hills with pastures rich in wild flowers – narcissi, snowdrops, cowslips, wild daffodils and violets in spring, autumn crocuses, dianthus (maiden pink) and spiraea. In May and early June the trees take on a dozen tints of green, which turn into shades of brown, russet red and yellow in September and October.

The Dordogne river coming into Corrèze from the north-east swells into a series of five placid lakes contained by hydro-electric dams until it reaches Argentat. They form a giant water stairway 100km long and have become part of the countryside except in the middle of dry summers when they sink to eroded slopes. There are some magnificent views near to them.

South of Brive is the Corrèze Causse (limestone plateau) and fruit is grown in the fertile valleys. It is sheep country, too, and geese are also kept for *confits d'oie* and *foie gras*. Walnut plantations are increasing after some years of neglect; so are truffle oak plantations, to raise supplies of this underground fungus with a price rivalling gold (*see* Food, page 16).

Down here are some delightful places to discover, like Collonges-la-Rouge and Turenne, and some beautiful secondary roads. But it is in the north and east of Corrèze that you find the secret world of lanes and hamlets where getting lost is a delight. Here you will discover a truly unknown area of France.

HOW TO GO

AIR

Bordeaux in Gironde is the major international airport of the south-west.

London Heathrow–Bordeaux (Air France, British Airways).

London Gatwick–Bordeaux (Euro Express – seasonal).

RAIL

TGV high-speed trains Paris–Bordeaux.

French Motorail car-carrying trains: Boulogne–Brive (9½ hours), Bordeaux (11 hours) – both seasonal; Paris (Austerlitz)–Brive (4½ hours); Bordeaux (6½ hours); Lille (Seclin)–Brive (9½ hours), seasonal.

ROAD

Motorways from just outside Boulogne/Calais/Dunkerque right through to Bordeaux via Paris.

Leave motorway at Poitiers, take N145, then N147 to Limoges. Then D704, D705 to Périgueux or N20 to Brive.

FOOD

It was late September as we drove under the stone gateway of the beautiful bastide (fortified village) of Monpazier, and summer visitors had fled. We had hardly seen a foreign or even Parisian car in a day of wandering the by-roads. But here parked cars almost jammed the narrow streets. We discovered why as soon as we turned into the main square where the last of the summer sun lit the ancient honey-coloured houses and squat arched arcades. They were holding a market for *cèpes* – those fragrant, fleshy fungi which add such subtle flavour to the simplest dishes. Restaurant chefs and hotel patrons had come from afar to buy. There were big baskets, wooden boxes, little cardboard fruit boxes and even small bags offered by old ladies and young boys. Expert eyes and fingers tested the quality of each *cèpe*. When few were left, we bought a handful from a delighted lad.

Back in our *gîte* we cooked them a local way, dipped in grape juice and simmered in oil with bacon and garlic.

'You should come here in winter when they sell truffles,' they told me in Monpazier's Hôtel de France, which was built about 1284 but which I have known only since 1953.

I have done better than that. I have been to the great Sarlat market when the truffles have come rolling in. I am happy to say that I am old enough to have eaten in the Dordogne when they served whole truffles simply wrapped in salted pork and paper in cinders, and also stuffed into slices of roast beef which were then braised in Madeira wine and served with slices of *foie gras* fried in butter, and tartlets filled with truffles in sauce. In cheapish restaurants they even used to serve potato croquettes dotted with chopped truffles, and, in Sarlat, *confit* of goose was served with sliced potatoes layered alternatively with truffles, and then fried in goose fat. They also stuffed eggs with truffles as a cocktail snack. You can still get all these dishes in very expensive restaurants but truffles are now so outrageously expensive that most people have to be content with pieces of truffle in pâtés or omelettes.

There are two reasons why a lot of people go without *foie gras*, the liver of fat goose, these days. Some object to the way the geese are 'force fed'. Others simply cannot afford it, except on special occasions. But there are plenty of superb dishes of goose, duck and chickens at down-to-earth prices. Sarlat potatoes are excellent layered with garlic instead of truffles, as are the salads served with chopped walnuts and dressed with walnut oil.

Goose, duck and chicken, with more turkey these days, are still the main sources of meat, and goose and duck fat continue to be used in preference to butter, lard or oil. (Walnut oil is now too expensive to use for cooking.) Even omelettes are often cooked in goose fat. If self-catering in Dordogne, you can buy goose fat by weight in butchers or in tins from charcuteries or some supermarkets. *Confits* of goose and duck are delicious. Joints of the poultry are conserved in their own fat and you can buy them in glass jars or tins. They are used in numerous recipes, but are excellent fried in their own fat, which is then used to fry or bake slices of potato. To counter the richness, eat it with a Périgourdine salad sprinkled with chopped walnuts and dressed with walnut oil mixed with a little white wine. You can use almost anything green – green beans, curly endive, lettuce, cooked globe artichoke hearts, cooked asparagus, even dandelion leaves if you like their mustardy taste.

There are some excellent fungi in the Dordogne beside the truffle. *Cèpes* are superb when fresh but add flavour to many dishes out of season when tinned. There is a dried version, but I personally have not mastered the art of cooking them. *Cèpes* are found often under chestnut trees. Crinkly *morilles*, which come in spring and have the most beautifully delicate flavour of all fungi, are found more frequently in the hills of the Corrèze. An unusual but delicious fungus you could probably find in Sarlat market is *oranges de César*. It is moistened with grape juice, then grilled for four to five minutes and served painted with walnut oil. A delicate pinkish meadow mushroom called *rosés des prés* is cooked in goose fat with sliced potato, garlic and parsley.

The great gourmet food writer, Curnonsky, 'Prince of Gastronomes', made a pun on the motto *'Sans Peur et Sans Reproche'* (without fear or reproach) saying that Périgord was *'Sans Beurre et Sans Reproche'* (without butter or reproach). He also said that truffle was a word never uttered by a gastronome without touching his hat. It was believed to be the food of love, like caviar and oysters. Curnonsky said that it was not a definite love potion but 'it can make a woman more loving and a man more loveable'.

Pigs were used for centuries to sniff out truffles from under the ground and a few are still trained to do so, but it is difficult to get them to release their prize before they eat it. Dogs have proved more helpful if given an occasional titbit. When November comes you can see farmers setting out on bicycles or mopeds with a dog sitting in the basket or running alongside. They are making for their own secret truffle patch in oakwoods, and they can spot where the 'black diamond' is growing by the dying grass. There are more than thirty varieties of truffle. The average weight is 100g, the biggest recorded weighed a kilo. They appear in the markets of Sarlat, Périgueux, Terrasson, Thiviers and Montignac in early December and are at their best at Christmas. Most of those used in the kitchen are tinned in Madeira wine or cognac and the liquid (truffle juice) is used for cooking, especially in sauce Périgueux, which is superb with steak, roast beef, game and poultry, particularly guinea fowl (*pintandeau*). Cook three chopped shallots and a big sliced onion in goose or duck fat until soft, then stir in 15g flour and cook until the liquid is slightly brown. Next stir in ⅓ litre of white wine, 1 litre of strong stock, salt and pepper. Simmer until reduced by half (about an hour). Add truffle juice, then 30–60g of thinly sliced truffles and simmer for three to four minutes.

Pâtés can be superb in Dordogne. Cheaper pâtés often have specks of truffle cutaways from other dishes. Anything marked 'with truffle juice' just contains the liquid from the tin. In *very* cheap 'truffled' pâtés, a black fungus called *trompettes de la morte* may have been substituted and it doesn't help.

Apart from in the forests of western Dordogne, there is little wild game left in Dordogne other than hare and pheasant. Most game served is domesticated. Boar are kept in pens on farms, and pheasant and quail carefully reared, so there are plenty of game pâtés – *pâté de sanglier* (boar), *de marcassin* (young boar), *de faisan* (pheasant), *de caille* (quail), as well as pigeon, *lapin* (rabbit), *lapereau* (young rabbit) and *lièvre* (hare).

One of the oldest sayings in Périgord is that if you have a neck of goose, a loaf of bread and a bottle of wine, you can invite your neighbour to a feast. *Cou d'oie*, stuffed neck of goose, is one of those peasant dishes which have become a gourmet's delight. The peasants stuffed it with chitterlings of the bird; now it is most often stuffed with chopped pork and duck liver or even *foie gras*, and the gastronomic version has truffles added. It is boiled, and usually served cold and sliced as a starter or between-meal snack. *Rillettes* are made with shredded pork, as in most of France, and served on unbuttered toast. *Rilles d'oie* are the same, but made of shredded goose.

When I first knew the Dordogne, soup was served midday and in the evenings with every menu in restaurants and even for breakfast in some private houses. The main meal in remoter villages was often simply a huge bowl of soup-stew with bread. In poorer houses meat and vegetable stock was poured over bread.

Tourain périgourdin is onion soup containing tomatoes and egg yolks. Grated cheese may be added. *Sobronade* is a 'whole-meal' soup. It includes fresh and salt pork and often bacon in large dice, simmered for a long time with whatever vegetables are in the market, especially white beans, plus turnips, carrots, celery and onions with garlic and assorted herbs, and then served over bread slices. The beans make it thick.

Jerusalem artichokes are grown around Bergerac – fairly rare in France.

Walnuts have always been a great crop in Dordogne, Corrèze and Lot, and only last year I saw a farmer's wife using a little hand machine in her barn to make walnut oil. In autumn you can still see older ladies sitting outside cottages with a tray of walnuts and a mallet, tapping the nuts open and extracting the walnuts. It is important to keep the walnut whole. Broken nuts fetch less than half the price of whole ones. Most of these walnuts are of a variety called *Corne*, which stay whole when cracked. *Grandjeu* are usually sold broken for making cakes or used for oil pressing. The remains after pressing, called *pain de noix*, are used for cattle feed. *Franquette* nuts are now seen in walnut plantations and used for all purposes. Once the walnut wood was used for rifle butts. Now it is prized for furniture veneers. A liqueur is also made from walnuts. It grows on you.

Walnuts are harvested in October and November and special walnut markets are held then and in early December. Brantôme has one on Friday, Ribérac on Wednesday; Montignac has a walnut and chestnut market on Wednesday. Monpazier has a chestnut market on Thursday and Sunday morning, Villefranche-du-Périgord on Saturday.

Chestnuts were once vital to the villages of Dordogne and Corrèze. The peasants here ground them into flour. Now they are eaten more frequently in Corrèze, where they are part of many local recipes. Most are *châtaignes*, segmented, not the dessert *marrons*. The wood is used extensively for furniture in France.

Dordogne is also the main centre, with the Loiret, for hazelnuts (*noisettes*), which produce a lovely aromatic oil. They are also used in nut and raisin bread, usually made with rye flour. Nuts are used greatly in making gâteaux. Sarlat has a tasty rum cake, *cajasse sarladaise*.

Les merveilles (sweet fritters) were traditionally eaten hot or cold on Shrove Tuesday, but are now served more frequently.

Dordogne produces a lot of fruit – *Reinette* apples, which have survived the invasion of Golden Delicious from the USA, peaches, pears, apricots and plums (dessert – not the prune plums grown in the Loire valley and around Agen). Dordogne is now the biggest producer of strawberries in France, growing more than forty per cent. Vergt, 20km south of Périgueux, is the main centre. You get them forced under plastic in March, but the peak period is May and June, and sometimes a second crop comes in October. Corrèze grows *Reinette* apples, *Reines-Claudes* and *prune-de-Vars* plums, raspberries (peak in June, July) and strawberries. In woods around August or September you will find lovely bilberries called *myrtilles*.

Dordogne produces little cheese. Most local cheeses have disappeared, including, I believe, Cubjac, made usually from a mixture of goats' and cows' milk, which I have not seen for years. A good but rare cheese is Abbey d'Echourgnac, a mild, fruity cow's cheese made by Trappist monks at their abbey at Montpon-sur-l'Isle. Corrèze has an unusual sheep's milk cheese, Tomme de Brach.

Some classic dishes of Périgord do still contain truffles. *Poularde à la périgourdine* is chicken stuffed with *foie gras* and truffles, doused in Cognac. *Poularde truffé à la périgourdine* has certainly passed out of my life and that of everyone I know. It takes several days to make because the chicken, stuffed with *foie gras* and truffles, is left for days in an earthenware jar covered with truffle peelings so that they can perfume the meat. One dish which I have had lately, however, is *Poulet sauté à la Périgord*, a young chicken cut up and fried with sliced truffles.

Corrèze and Dordogne both claim a superb *ballottine* of hare. In the Dordogne it is called *ballottine de lièvre à la périgourdine* and in Corrèze, where it probably originated, *lièvre à la royale*, meaning that it is fit for a king. The hare is boned, stuffed with hare heart, liver, leg meat, fat pork, chopped onions and bread-crumbs mixed with *foie gras*, soaked in Cognac, rolled, and cooked slowly in white wine. It is served hot. Other hare, rabbit and chicken *ballottines* are served cold, and are often bought sliced from *charcuteries*.

Corrèze produces excellent pork. Roast pork (*carré de porc à la limousine*) is served with red cabbage braised with chestnuts.

(Boiled chestnuts are called *boursadas*, grilled are called *chauvnets*.) However Corrèze is known especially for its beef from cattle of the Millevaches Plateau, which are a cross between a local breed and English Durham beef cattle. Corrèze is part of old Limousin and that has been an important area for meat for many centuries. It has had a Butchers' Corporation since AD930, and since the seventeenth century the butchers have been charged with guarding the safety of visitors. But Plateau de Millevaches does not mean the plateau of a thousand cows, but of many rivers.

In Dordogne there are inevitably some excellent restaurants serving expensive meals, like the Moulin du Roc at Champagnac de Belair, Moulin de l'Abbaye at Brantôme and Vieux Logis at Trémolat. But it has a big choice of local restaurants offering three- or four-course meals with hearty Perigordian portions for around 60F (just flip through the *Logis de France* list). There is hardly a big village without at least one good restaurant. Off the tourist tracks there are scores offering full-blown meals with choice for 50F or even under. One reader wrote to say that I was exaggerating and that it is not possible now to find a full meal under 75F. He has not explored enough. Even in big towns like Bergerac you can find them. While we were waiting for our long-suffering car to be repaired in 1988, we had a meal in a little restaurant called Chez Germaine on boulevard Chanzy, where Germaine herself cooks and serves. All our fellow eaters were locals. First course was *crudités* and *charcuterie* – a loaded table from which you helped yourself to cold meats, sausage and home-made pâté. Then a huge tureen of vegetable soup was placed on our table with a litre of Bergerac wine. When we finished the wine another litre arrived. The main course was a plate laden with lamb and four vegetables served in help-yourself dishes. A good choice of cheese followed, then a home-made gâteau and coffee. The price was 49F each. I understand that by 1990 the prices had shot up to 59F!

Mind you, in the cheaper restaurants there are substitutes for truffles. *Ris de veau aux truffes* (sweetbreads braised with truffles and mushrooms in white wine and cream) may become '*aux tomates*', with tomatoes substituted.

WINE

The improvement in the wines of Bergerac has been one of the delights of wine-drinkers in the last decade. Modern methods have had a revolutionary effect on some of the white wines, and the reds are still improving through copying from nearby Bordeaux the system of bringing in a high percentage of new barrels every year. Some old Bergerac winemakers used to *boast* that their barrels were a hundred years old. As some of the wines, such as Pécharmont from the gravelly hills north of Bergerac, are kept in cask for up to three years, the tannin in them was formidable and would not soften much even after ten years. It killed the fruity flavour completely.

One of the makers largely responsible for the welcome revolution is Pierre-Jean Sardoux, who makes the delicious Château Court-les-Mûts Bergerac and also Saussignac wines at Razac-de-Saussignac, south of Bergerac. He is a renowned oenologist from the Wine Institute of Bordeaux and uses the modern methods of vinification in lined metal tanks and low-temperature fermentation which have improved red wines in many parts of the world. His vines are old and he uses a lot of the Merlot grape popular in Bordeaux (especially St Émilion) to give his wines a plummy, velvety taste. He matures them for eighteen months in oak barrels which are new every year – just like those in Château Margaux, Lafite-Rothschild and the other Premier Grand Cru wines of Bordeaux. The wine keeps for six to seven years, by which time it is soft and full. His dry white wine contains 70 per cent Sémillon grape, which gives it a fruity, soft taste, and he makes a rare white Saussignac Moelleux that is rich, sweet and strong.

Two others who have done a lot to improve Bergerac wines are English – Nicholas and Hugh Ryman. Nicholas Ryman sold his big stationers empire in England before he was forty in order to achieve his ambition to make wine in France. He bought the lovely but decaying Château La Jaubertie at Colombier, near to Monbazillac, 8km south of Bergerac (*see* Monbazillac, page 139) knowing nothing about winemaking. Now he produces what most people believe to be the best white wine in Bergerac – Château La Jaubertie Bergerac sec (superbly fruity with a heady bouquet from the addition of Muscadelle grapes); an extra fruity and perfumed Sauvignon, softened by adding Sémillon grapes, and so popular that it is not easy to buy; and a delicious fruity, highly perfumed aromatic white made from old Muscadelle grapes which cannot be made every year. His whites and reds have won gold, silver and bronze medals at the great Maçon Wine Fair. The fruity, mouth-filling reds are far above most Bergerac reds I have drunk, except those of Sardoux. Modern metal *cuvés* are used for making them and a high percentage of barrels are changed each year. His latest red, made by his new winemaker Charles Wilson, is Réserve Colombier, made of 95 per cent Merlot grapes.

Hugh Ryman, Nicholas's son, learned winemaking at the University of Bordeaux, in Burgundy and in Australia with Alan Clother, said by many to be 'the best white-winemaker in the world'. He made Jaubertie white until recently, is now a consultant winemaker and a *négociant* (wholesaler) and *éleveur* (maturer). He has made and improved many country wines all over south-west France. Look out for his Bergerac Sec Château Haut Peygonthier, made by the modern low-temperature method from 70 per cent Sémillon and 30 per cent Muscadelle – clean, fruity, aromatic and quite rich.

Flag-carrier of Bergerac reds for years and still very palatable is Château de Tiregand, a Pécharmant Bergerac made by the Count and Countess of St-Exupéry. Pécharmant is rich in colour, almost purple when young, and at its best when four to six years old. Red Bergerac, which has twice won gold medals at Maçon, is made at the thirteenth-century Château de Panisseau. In 1363, when the English owned Aquitaine, the Seigneur de Panisseau paid homage for his title to the Prince of Wales. Well worth visiting to taste the wine. Take D936 west from Bergerac towards Bordeaux for 5km, left on D16 to Cunèges, then follow signs for 2km to Panisseau.

You can also taste at Château La Jaubertie at Colombier (take N21 south-east from Bergerac, at 8km is a sign right to Colombier with vineyard name); at Château Court-les-Mûts at Razac-de-Saussignac (D936 west from Bergerac, left on D4 at Gardonne, right on D14, then lane left); and at Château de Tiregand, Creysse (D660 from Bergerac towards Lalinde; as board of Creysse village appears, turn left under railway bridge).

Monbazillac wine is an underestimated sweet wine, once passed off as Sauternes, though it is often richer and stronger. Its grape varieties are the same as Sauternes – Sémillon for flavour and richness, Sauvignon for body, Muscadelle for aroma. Most people drink it young, when it is light gold in colour, very cold, as an aperitif or with fruity desserts, but it is well worth keeping five to ten years and drinking with a rich pâté (or *foie gras*!) and superb with strawberries. Above Monbazillac village, in the vineyards, is the superb Château de Monbazillac (*see* page 138). For the excellent Cave-Cooperative which offers tastings, take D933 south from Bergerac past St Laurent. Caves are on the right. They have Château de Monbazillac wines, a Pécharmant from Château La Renaudie, Bergerac white, red and rosé, and a champagne-method *pétillant* (gently sparkling) white called Festival. You pay around £1.50 for a half-hour tour of the caves and tasting in the seventeenth-century *chais*. There is a restaurant and wine shop.

Rosette, a semi-sweet white wine from slopes north of Bergerac, is fragrant, quite heavy and goes well with poultry or fish in rich sauces. Almost all is drunk around Bergerac.

Montravel is in the Dordogne and its reds are sold as Bergerac, but it is only 10km east of St Émilion, is more like a Bordeaux and is good value. Among its whites, Côtes de Montravel are sweet wines very like good sweeter Bordeaux wines; its ordinary Montravel whites are dry, *demi-sec* or sweet.

Vins de Pays de la Dordogne are simple local wines. Much is produced around Sarlat. The red can be fruity and attractive. The dry white is crisp but sometimes acidic. I used to believe that no wine came from Corrèze. But that kind of judgement is always a mistake in France. Commander Anthony Hogg, one of the original Peter Dominic team, once found me a vineyard in Paris! Beaulieu-sur-Dordogne, it seems, produces a sweet white wine which is said to be a poor version of Jura's *vin de paille* (straw-coloured wine). The grapes are dried on beds of straw.

HISTORY AND ART

Les Eyzies-de-Tayac has the right to call itself 'The Capital of Prehistory'. Its caves have revealed more evidence of our prehistoric ancestors of 150,000 to 40,000 years ago than anywhere else in the world. In fact, the rediscovered caves around the Dordogne and Vézère rivers have given us the first real picture of early man's way of living, the tools and weapons he constructed in bone and stone, the jewellery he made, the mammoth elephants, horses, oxen, bison, bears, deer, rhinoceroses and reindeer he hunted. Human and animal skeletons have been found and remarkable engravings, paintings and sculptures on the cave walls. Some of these are quite beautiful. The *Michelin Green Guide* to the Dordogne gives a good beginners guide to prehistory, and the museum at Les Eyzies (Musée National de Préhistoire, *see* Sites, page 60) is fascinating.

These caves were certainly known to man later in the Dark Ages and Middle Ages, and used as shelters when tribes like the Visigoths and Franks invaded, and when the rival Capet and

Ancient drystone huts near Sireuil

Plantagenet families were fighting for power in France. Again, in the Hundred Years War between the French and English (1337–1453), people sought refuge in them from the pillaging troops of both sides, and especially from the mercenary barons whose armies called 'routiers' fought and ransacked where they could find most loot. In the Wars of Religion, too, people hid in the caves from both Huguenot bands and the particularly ruthless Catholic Leaguers.

For centuries after, many of the caves were forgotten. Others were simply regarded as dark, wet and useless, or people were afraid to go into them because of legends which had grown up around them.

In 1863, the archaeologist Édouard Lartet and his British banker friend Henry Christy discovered a carved and chiselled mammoth's tusk in the village of La Madeleine, upstream from Les Eyzies on the Vézère river, which suggested the existence of 'Magdelanian' man living around 40,000 years ago. Lartet made more digs and discoveries in the Vézère valley. Five years later the remains of a family which had lived about 35,000 years ago were found at a place called Cro-Magnon by workmen laying the Périgueux–Agen railway. These remains were called 'Cro-Magnon' man. 'Mousteranian' man, who lived about 150,000 years ago, was found at Le Moustier, also upstream from Les Eyzies on the river Vézère.

It must have been hell to live in the Dordogne through the Middle Ages, despite the beauty and fertility of the land. Wars continued for over 300 years from the early twelfth century, and, in the sixteenth century, little more than a hundred years after the English had been driven from France, the Religious Wars between Catholics and Protestants, with all their viciousness and destruction, came to the Dordogne. In all these wars the ordinary people were the true sufferers. Crops were stolen by the armies as soon as they were harvested, and cattle and poultry were just taken, slaughtered and eaten. Women were raped. Homes were looted and burned down.

People within castles, or those who could reach them in an emergency, were safest. In the Hundred Years War some lucky peasants were able to live in the new fortified villages, bastides. The first of these seem to have been built by Henry Plantagenet

(Henry III of England) in the 1250s at Lalinde on the Dordogne river and Villefranche-du-Périgord. The idea was to persuade people to stay on the land and work it, despite the hazards, and to give them a chance to market their produce. Peasants who moved into the fortified bastides were rewarded with land outside to cultivate and a house inside, protection (which sometimes failed) and exemption from military service. The towns were given rights to hold markets and power over local villages. They were also used by companies of soldiers moving around the country as safe overnight stops.

English and French bastides were built on similar plans – a square or rectangle with streets crossing at right angles and a centre square with a market hall surrounded by houses with arcades below them which were used as shops. The whole was protected by thick walls with towers and fortified gateways and the church was usually fortified, often with four crenellated towers, as a final refuge if the enemy got into the town. Nevertheless, bastides were taken and changed hands, as were castles, and very often the soldiers and peasants were just slaughtered by the enemy. The only prisoners taken were lords, knights and commanders who might fetch a ransom. Bastides such as Monpazier and Domme, fought over fiercely in the Hundred Years War and Wars of Religion, are now beautiful tourist attractions, and peaceful out of season or in the evenings when the day visitors have gone. Stay overnight to appreciate them best.

In the early Middle Ages the Capetians, Frankish kings, were ambitious to take over most of the area we now call France, and the local rulers, such as the Counts of Anjou and Dukes in the south-west, were determined to keep their land and their power.

France seemed to have succeeded in taking over the south-west in 1137, when Prince Louis, son of the King of France, married the beautiful, intelligent, fifteen-year-old Eleanor of Aquitaine. Her dowry was the Duchy of Guyenne, Périgord, Limousin, Poitou, Angoumois, Saintonge, Gascony, the Auvergne and the County of Toulouse. But Louis, who was soon crowned Louis VII, was extremely pious and dull. She loved having fun, patronized the arts and liked to surround herself with troubadours. 'I have married a monk,' she said, despite their two daughters, and, in fact, Louis behaved as much like a monk as a King of France could do. He liked to dress in the simplest of clothes, to eat the simplest food and little of it, and spent hours on his knees in prayer. When he went on a crusade for two and a half years, she insisted on going with him. They soon began to live apart in the Holy Land and he accused her of having *affaires*. When he got back to France he set about getting rid of her. The French politicians sided with him. They wanted a male heir and Eleanor had committed the crime of having two girls. An Ecclesiastical Court was called and it announced that their wedding had been illegal under Church law because Louis and Eleanor were too closely related. The Pope annulled their marriage. Louis was so pleased to be rid of her that he agreed not only to her regaining her freedom but also her land.

She was thirty, still beautiful and rich. Many men were after her, including the King's younger brother. There were two kidnap attempts. But she knew who she wanted – a lusty, handsome, ginger-headed young man of nineteen whom she had spotted when his mother had brought him to the French court hoping to get him betrothed to Eleanor's fourteen-year-old daughter. He was Henry Plantagenet, already Duke of Normandy, Count of Anjou and Lord of Maine and Touraine. He was also heir to the English throne. Eleanor married him eight months after her divorce. Two years later he became King of England. His empire stretched from the Scottish borders to the Pyrenees and he ruled more land in France than the King of France did.

They were happy together at first. Eleanor indulged her love of parties and they held one to which troubadours came from many parts of Europe – the first European pop concert! Eleanor and Henry had five sons (one of whom died) and five daughters, but each still found time for *affaires* on the side. Henry fell for the Fair Rosamund and they had a child. He accused Eleanor of sleeping with a troubadour. They had an acrimonious row. Henry was an able king and military commander, and a clearheaded but unprincipled politician, but he had the Plantagenet quick temper. He confined Eleanor to a castle. Her dignity was very badly hurt and she turned her sons against him.

Henry had named his eldest son – also called Henry, but known as Henry Courtmantel because he started a fashion for short jackets – as his associate and heir. Eleanor's favourite was Richard Lionheart. She incited them both to rebel against their father, to the joy of both the clever new French King, Philippe-Auguste, and the King of Scotland. Henry Courtmantel committed the sacrilege of robbing abbeys and the rich shrine of Rocamadour to pay his army. He became very ill and was convinced he had been struck by the wrath of God. He fled to Martel in Quercy where he died alone, having fallen on a bed of cinders. Richard joined with the French King to fight his father, and finally so did John, the youngest son and Henry's favourite. Henry was forced to sign a very humiliating treaty. Tired, ill and disillusioned, he died in sorrow.

Richard became King of England and was soon fighting, and mainly beating, his 'ally', the King of France. But Richard was killed by an arrow at a minor siege in 1199 and his weaker brother John was no match for the cunning Philippe-Auguste. By 1259 the English had lost Poitou, but kept the Dukedom of Guyenne, holding the south part of Périgord.

Edward I's bastides protected the English positions and the French quickly started to build their own. Meanwhile, the ambitious, brutal and fanatical Simon de Montfort was burning and knocking down castles for the Pope on the excuse that their owners were sympathetic to the Albigensian sect, originally called Cathars. These people called themselves Christians but hoped to find perfection here on earth, not in some future heaven. They said that material things did not matter. Albi was their main centre. They lived in peace with Catholics, but not with the church authorities or the Pope, whose authority they denied. They were called heretics and St Bernard set out to reconvert them to Catholicism. He started in Sarlat in 1147, where he is claimed to have cured many people of the plague but failed to convert the heretics. French peasants preferred the promise of Heaven on Earth to Pie in the Sky and the Albigensian faith spread through southern France.

In 1208, Pope Innocent III decided that these heretics who defied him must be wiped out. As the Instrument of God he made an odd choice – Simon de Montfort, who was an Anglo-

Norman, Viscount of Carcassonne and Béziers, and Earl of Leicester through an astute marriage. He was brutal with a total disregard for human life and property and desperately ambitious. He killed men, women and children, destroying their homes, and needed no evidence to accuse owners of manor houses or castles of being sect-sympathizers. This way he seized Domme, Beynac and Castelnaud châteaux and the château now called Montfort in one year. He wanted to be Count of Toulouse and besieged the city. A local stonemason recognized him and threw a boulder which smashed in his head and killed him. But the Pope's campaign continued until the Albigensians were virtually wiped out – even the children.

Intermittent fighting between the French and English continued in the south-west until the line of Capetian Kings died out in 1328. A Valois, Philip VI, took the throne. But Edward III of England was a Valois, too, and as his mother was the daughter of the King of France, Philip the Fair, he, too, claimed the French throne. Philip VI was Philip the Fair's younger brother. Edward invaded France, defeated the French comprehensively at Crécy in 1346 and took Calais. The war reached the Dordogne and Corrèze, and the English took Tulle and then Domme. It is strange now to think how important Domme was for so long. Then the Black Death swept Europe and the fighting ceased as tens of thousands died.

Wine caused the fresh outbreak of fighting. In 1355, the Gascons of Bordeaux, whose lifeblood was exporting wine to England, were hard pressed by the French and appealed for English help. It was just the excuse the brilliant soldier the Black Prince, eldest son of Edward III, needed to land in Bordeaux. Next year he beat the French armies at Poitiers and took King John II of France prisoner. The Périgourdins decided that backing England was their best bet and the merchants of Sarlat tried to hand over their town to the English. Under the Treaty of Bretigny, which released the French King, the English got all of Périgord, including Sarlat. Edward gave up his claim to the French throne.

Ten years later the great Breton soldier Bertrand Du Guesclin, who had abandoned Brittany to become Marshal of France, Brittany's enemy, renewed the fighting by attacking the

English with fresh troops. The Black Prince's army had been decimated by disease and dysentery while fighting in Spain, so John of Gaunt, Duke of Lancaster, brought an army of 30,000 men to join the Duke of Brittany to fight Du Guesclin in the Dordogne. When he reached there, his force was down to less than 7000 men through disease and starvation. Much of their march had been through enemy territory. The Duke of Brittany took one look at them and went home. Aquitaine was soon under French rule. The following century Henry V revived the English claim to Périgord and to the throne of France. His claim rested on the slim evidence that Edward III was his great-grandfather. He sailed in 1415, took Harfleur, then won one of the greatest military victories in history at Agincourt when his small army, exhausted and racked with sickness, beat a fresh and fit French army three times its size – the last great victory of English archers before men with guns took over. Henry and Charles VI of France signed one of those treaties which was to bring 'perpetual peace' – the Treaty of Troyes. Henry married Catherine de Valois, the French King's daughter, and was made heir to the French throne by Charles, who was already mentally unbalanced.

Henry and Charles both died within two years. Henry's infant son was declared King of France and England. The Duke of Bedford was made Regent of France. Charles' son, the Dauphin, the real heir to the French throne, announced himself King Charles VII but stayed in virtual exile in the Loire and was called scathingly in Paris 'King of Bourges'. His father had been mentally ill for years. He himself was tormented by indecision and doubts. His mother, Queen Isabeau, a Bavarian, was sensuous and known to be unfaithful to her husband, even with his own brother, the flamboyant Duke of Orléans, so the Dauphin even doubted that he was the true heir of France.

Then came the remarkable peasant girl Joan of Arc who told him that God had sent voices to tell her that he *was* the true heir of France and that she was to raise an army to save France. She rallied both him and the French. With the help of Jean Dunois – 'the Bastard of Orléans', who had just given the Dauphin his first victory over the English at Montargis – she relieved Orléans and beat the English at Patay. After her disgraceful execution by the English and the French clergy, Dunois played a major part in driving the English from Paris, Normandy and finally south-west France. The last battle was in Périgord at Castillon. John Talbot, Earl of Shrewsbury, a great soldier and victor of forty battles, but now seventy-five years of age, marched to relieve the besieged town. He fell for a false story that the French were retreating, was caught in a trap and defeated. Talbot's horse fell and trapped his leg and a Frenchman put an axe through his head – thus depriving himself of a lucrative ransom. At least Talbot still has an excellent Grand Cru Bordeaux wine named after him.

Though the Hundred Years War was over, much of France was destitute. Wolves roamed in city streets, epidemics spread, only a handful of people were left in many towns, and robberbands of former soldiers roamed the countryside looting whatever was left. Périgord was in ruins, Quercy (Lot) was even worse. Three quarters of their churches were abandoned. People from Languedoc and Auvergne were brought in to populate almost abandoned towns and villages.

It took France nearly a hundred years to recover fully. Then the Wars of Religion started in 1562 between the Calvinist Protestants and Catholics. The people of Périgord and Quercy were generally Protestant, mostly because of poverty but also because of the powerful influence in the south-west of the Protestant Jeanne d'Albret, Queen of Navarre, and her son Henri of Navarre. One of his companions was the great Protestant captain Geoffroi de Vivans, born in Castelnaud in 1543. Another was Henri de la Tour d'Auvergne of the powerful Turenne family.

Two kings in succession were children. François II, officially married to the child Mary Stuart (Mary, Queen of Scots), was fifteen and ailing. The extreme Catholic family, the Guises, related to Mary Stuart, ran the country. They wanted the French throne for themselves and they were fanatically antiProtestant. Then François died. His successor, Charles IX, was ten years old. His mother, Catherine de' Medici, became Regent. Although she was a Catholic, she tolerated Protestants at Court and the Catholic nobility, especially the Guises, plotted to get rid of her. The Duke de Guise and his private army came upon a Protestant prayer-meeting, set upon the Protestants, and killed or wounded 153 of them. The Religious Wars started, with an appalling ferocity. In Paris, the Catholics burned down the Protestants' houses. In the south, the Protestants destroyed and looted the churches.

Vivans, who got into Domme on the Dordogne in spite of its apparently impregnable defences, gratuitously destroyed its church. But far worse things were happening to the ordinary people as soldiers once again pillaged, looted, murdered, destroyed and raped, this time in the name of religion, not nationalism. As usual, only captured leaders were well treated.

'Perhaps at the outset men fought for their faith,' wrote André Maurois. 'Very soon indeed they were fighting for the fun of it.' But not the leaders – they fought as usual for power.

Catherine de' Medici hoped to curb the power of the Guises and ultimately solve the argument by marrying her daughter Marguerite to the popular young Protestant leader Henri of Navarre, who was of royal blood. The wrath of the Catholics was truly roused. By the time the wedding day came, Guise persuaded her and young King Charles that this would put fatal power in the hands of the Protestants. She joined with Guise in a terrible plot. All the Protestant leaders and important followers were invited to Paris for the wedding on St Bartholomew's Day 1572. Guise had drawn up a list of Protestants not only in Paris but all over France. After the wedding, several thousand Protestants were murdered by Guise's gangs in Paris alone – including great men like Rochefoucaud and Caumont-la-Force. In other parts of France many were murdered. Henri of Navarre alone was spared, but shut up in the Louvre Palace. The Prince of Condé smelt a rat and did not go to Paris. King Philippe of Spain sent congratulations: 'This is one of the greatest joys of my whole life.' The Pope had a *Te Deum* sung. Queen Elizabeth of England went into mourning.

In the south, from Périgord to Béarn and the Pyrenean Spanish frontier the Protestants regrouped. They set up a united administration. Béarn formed a Protestant Republic.

One very dark, frosty night Henri of Navarre slipped out of Paris and rejoined the Protestant armies in the south. He became their commander. King Charles was struck by sickness and depression and died. His younger brother, who had been elected King of Poland, returned to be Henri III of France. He was a playboy who wore bracelets, necklaces, perfumes and women's make-up, but he was also intelligent and liberal. He gave the Protestants 'places of refuge', freedom of worship and the right to any employment. He and Catherine tried to persuade Henri of Navarre to become Catholic. The Guises formed the extremist Catholic League, the most vicious and feared force in France's history. They forced Henri III to ban the Protestants. But soon fighting was going in three directions – between the Protestants, the League and the Royal Catholics. King Henri had Henri de Guise murdered. Then Henri III was killed by a fanatical monk, egged on by priests. Henri of Navarre was his heir, but a Protestant could not become King so he professed to become a Catholic – some say to grab the throne, others to unite France. 'Paris is worth a Mass,' he said. With his Edict of Nantes, he made the Protestant faith legal and he made France solvent. He was the most popular of all French kings – except with the big landowners and nobles, who were made to pay taxes, almost unknown previously. But he, too, was murdered, by a man who was a tool of the Jesuits.

For long after the Religious Wars, Périgord and its neighbour Quercy were again in a terrible state of poverty. Crippling rents demanded by landowners drove peasant families to near starvation. Landowners took two thirds of what the peasants produced. Families lived on maize or chestnut flour mixed with a little fat to make dumplings (*miques*). Harvest failures brought starvation and death. Dispossessed peasants tried to make a living in the forests as charcoal-burners or knife-grinders. Tax officials became corrupt again, lining their own pockets, and twice the Dordogne peasants (Croquants) revolted, gathering in the forests and marching against landowners and tax collectors, lynching some and destroying property.

In 1685, Louis XIV, influenced by his new wife and former mistress, Madame de Maintenon, who was herself under the influence of the Jesuits, revoked the Edict of Nantes, made the Protestant faith illegal again and started a bloody persecution which drove half a million Protestants fleeing to Holland, England, Germany and America. Louis' '*dragonnades*' were told to make life intolerable for Protestant sympathizers and to frighten them into becoming Catholics. They used every method, including public torture. France lost not only experienced soldiers, sailors, magistrates and businessmen but also, above all, skilled craftsmen who produced the communities' wealth, especially in Périgord, Bordeaux and the rest of the south-west. Bergerac lost half of its population. But Périgueux, which was mainly Catholic, thrived.

Most of the people of Périgord supported the Revolution in 1789. They were still desperately poor and downtrodden by landlords. They attacked castles, the rich abbeys and big churches, and looted manor houses. But the local clergy and village churches they left alone, for these were almost as poor as they were. They were still religious people. Over the door of Monpazier's old church they inscribed: 'The People of France recognize the existence of a Supreme Being and the immortality of the soul.' It was Rome and its wealth that they were still against.

But the Revolution did them little good. They remained desperately poor and Napoleon was able to recruit soldiers easily from the Dordogne. Some reached high rank. One Yrieux Daumesnil, born at Périgueux in 1776, and the son of a tailor, became a national hero under Napoleon. At sixteen he killed a soldier in a duel, fled to join his brother's regiment in Toulouse, fought in Spain and was forgiven after his return to Périgueux. A devoted admirer of Napoleon, he saved his hero's life four times in battle, three times at the battle of La Favorite. When in Egypt with Napoleon, he and some friends insulted some officers and, being rankers, were sentenced to death. Napoleon reprieved him but not his friends. His heroism was so great at the Battle of Aboukir that he was promoted to brigadier.

He fought at Austerlitz, Jena, Eylau and in Spain. At Eckmühl he had two horses killed under him and was promoted to colonel-major. At Wagram, his leg was so badly damaged that Napoleon's surgeon amputated it. Napoleon gave him a directorship of the Bank of France, a sixteen-year-old wife and command of Vincennes Château in Paris, a prison and huge armsstore.

When Napoleon was defeated, Vincennes had to be handed to the Allies under the Armistice agreement. Daumesnil refused, telling Marshal Blücker that he would give up the keys 'if you give me back my leg'. He withstood a 120-day siege, threatening to blow up the arms and a lot of Paris with them. So the Allies gave up and let France keep the arms-store.

François Fournier, son of a Sarlat bar owner, was an uncouth, brave thug. He called himself 'Fournier-Sarlovèze' for pride of his home town, but despite his bravery he was so overbearing that Napoleon refused to honour him. So he plotted against Napoleon who banished him to Sarlat. However, he was recalled when the Emperor ran short of officers, and once more behaved like a thug. He galloped into Salamanca Cathedral and right up to the altar on his horse, then broke down barricades of a convent, terrified the nuns, and sang mass in a bellowing voice. Nevertheless, he was made a general. During Napoleon's retreat from Moscow he charged a whole Cossack regiment with a small force but returned with gangrene in his feet from frost-bite. Napoleon made him a Baron of the Empire, and when the monarchy returned he was one of the few who succeeded in keeping his title.

The Dordogne people were loyal to France and the throne. They backed the ineffective kings of the nineteenth century and most supported the Emperor Napoleon III. Bergerac, whose people had changed from militant Protestants to Democratic Socialists, rebelled at having a Bonaparte dictator back. Napoleon's army put down the revolt and banished some Bergerac citizens to the French colonies. As one respected Bergerac man said to me recently: 'Now we save up our money to have just two weeks in Martinique.'

Another blow hit the Dordogne when coal replaced charcoal for iron and steel production and the forges closed. Peasants had tended their farms in summer, and in winter had felled forest oaks, made charcoal and smelted iron.

A further blow to the little towns came when Napoleon III abolished the customs duties which had protected French industry from foreign competition. People left for the factories of Paris and the big cities.

In the 1850s came the final blow. The aphid which destroys vines, phylloxera, spread from the Midi to Bordeaux and Bergerac, then to all Dordogne and Lot vineyards. Within a few years two thirds of the vineyards had ceased production. Wine production in Dordogne and Lot has never fully recovered but there has been a revolutionary resurgence in Bergerac in the last few years, with modern methods of vinification and good marketing making long-slumbering vineyards alive and successful.

After France fell in 1940, Dordogne was lucky enough to be in the unoccupied zone called 'Vichy France' because its puppet government was in Vichy. Refugees from heavily occupied areas, especially Belgium and Alsace–Lorraine, escaped over the border and hid in Dordogne and Lot, which became a great Resistance centre. The RAF used it as a dropping zone and arms and men were hidden in caves. St Céré, in Lot but near to the Dordogne river, was a major centre. Colonel Buckmaster, London organizer of the Resistance, set up a headquarters at the Hotel de Paris (now the Hotel Paris et Coq Arlequin) and 'dropped in' sometimes.

From Sarlat, 'Colonel Berger' ran the Resistance FFI (Free French Intelligence). He was the writer André Malraux, who had escaped from a prison camp and who, as Minister of Culture, did such a splendid job of restoring Sarlat (*see* page 50).

As explained in the Introduction, the Dordogne, like Lot and the Auvergne, was becoming derelict after the war. Very few young men returned. I have heard many Britons say since that tourists and old people retiring there have 'spoiled' it. Tell that to the people of Dordogne! They have not been so prosperous nor their land so well kept for centuries.

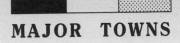
Bergerac

[MAP 2, page 196]

Bergerac is the biggest town on the Dordogne river. Although an important commercial centre, it is not pretty, but its attractions and atmosphere have grown on me and I thoroughly enjoy going there now.

If first impressions matter to you, come in from the south on the N21 Agen road over the Dordogne bridge. Then you will see low, red-roofed buildings along the river bank, which are only about 500 metres from the old port. From here, wines were exported via Libourne, and the trading barges were sailed and poled up and down the river before the railways came. If you come in from the north on the N21, you pass scruffy, depressing old industrial buildings, although the road does lead conveniently straight to place de la République, which is just a big car-park now. The east entrance along the D660, although it runs very close to the river, is cut off from it until the last little stretch by such atrocities as the barbed-wire compound that looks like a concentration camp, which was once an important gunpowder factory for the army. Now, I am told, it produces nitrocellulose for use in making films, paint, varnish and plastic.

Try to be in Bergerac on a Wednesday or Saturday morning. It is still a genuine, old-style agricultural market town, and the farmers bring in their produce and sell it direct to the public right in the shadow of the slender Gothic belltower of the Cathedral of Notre-Dame. Apart from superb vegetables and fruit, one can buy lovely farm-made duck *confit* in bottles and farm-made pâtés there. On the first and third Tuesday of the month live farm animals are brought to market. A good flea market is also held on the first Sunday in each month.

The port was very important for trading along the river (*see* Introduction, page 12). Wine was taken from here to Libourne to avoid Bordeaux, which was trying to kill all but its own export trade, even fiddling the size of barrels to beat Bergerac. Behind the port, you can get an idea of what Bergerac looked like in those days. Narrow streets are still bordered by some timber-framed houses, topped by corbelled towers and decorated with medieval and Renaissance bays.

In the seventeenth-century mansion of the Peyrarède family is a tobacco museum (Musée du Tabac). I lost interest in tobacco long since but this museum is fascinating because it shows you how the weed influenced manners and habits over five centuries, as well as its effect on economics and politics. The collection of snuff boxes and pipes in the museum is especially interesting.

The French take a more cavalier attitude to tobacco and its dangers than the British. Perhaps that is because tobacco is still a major industry, especially in the Dordogne, though its importance is dying gradually. (Our own Treasury in Britain might be sorely pressed if we all gave up smoking and paid no tax on cigarettes!) Bergerac has the only experimental Institute of Tobacco, but it looked overgrown and closed when I last passed it.

The local history museum is also in the Peyrarède mansion. You can visit the old St Jacques pilgrim church, but it was rather badly restored last century. Much of Bergerac was destroyed in the Religious Wars but happily the old Convent of Recollects, built in brick and stone over five centuries, survived and is now a Maison du Vin where wine-tastings are held in the vaulted cellars. The inner courtyard of the monastery, the old cloisters, has two fine galleries side by side – built in the fourteenth and sixteenth centuries – and from the beautifully decorated great hall on the first floor you can see far over the Monbazillac vineyards south of the town.

Behind the port in place de la Myrpe is a statue of a strange local hero – Cyrano de Bergerac. It was Edmond Rostand who made him famous in 1897 by writing a wildly melodramatic play in verse about a swordsman and poet who had such a big, ugly nose that he was insulted by men and spurned by women. He fought a thousand duels to defend his honour. The woman he loved, Roxane, spurned him so he wrote love-letters for a friend to send to her and woo her. In fact Cyrano de Bergerac lived from 1619–55, was a soldier and swordsman who was said to enjoy duelling very much, and was a *libertin* poet – a free-thinker in revolt against the orthodox beliefs of the Church. His main works – *Histoires Comiques des États de la Lune et du Soleil* – were satirical, almost lunatic descriptions of journeys to the moon and sun, heavily laced with satire against orthodox religion. The poems were said to have given Swift the idea for *Gulliver's Travels* and Voltaire for *Micromégas*. Cyrano was also renowned for his love-letters.

Long before Rostand wrote the play, the people of Bergerac had named a street after Cyrano; it is unfortunate that some Parisians insist that, as he went to school in Beauvais, he must have come from some place of little consequence, also called Bergerac, just outside Paris. The Périgord reply has been to use on posters his formidable nose appreciating the great 'nose' of good Bergerac wines.

The cathedral of Notre-Dame was built last century in Gothic style. Inside are an *Adoration of the Magi* by a Venetian painter Pordenone and an *Adoration of the Shepherds* attributed to a Milanese, Ferrari, student of da Vinci. Both are sixteenth century.

In the Religious Wars, Bergerac was the main centre in Périgord of Protestants, and Périgueux the capital of Catholicism – and neither has yet quite forgiven the other. The Protestants strengthened Bergerac's defence by pulling down most of the monasteries to use for stone fortifications. Later Richelieu had the ramparts knocked down again. When Louis XIV made Protestantism illegal again by revoking Henri IV's Edict of Nantes, the Protestants were persecuted terribly and at least half the people of Bergerac, especially the skilled craftsmen, fled to England or Holland. Bergerac almost died as a commercial town, but the refugees in Holland still wanted their beloved Bergerac wine and that trade, at least, continued.

It is not surprising that Bergerac has many good restaurants in all price ranges and that one of the very best is called Le

Cyrano. It has some good shops, too, and also has a big parachute-jumping school at the airfield for those who jump for fun.

TOURIST INFORMATION 97 rue Neuve-d'Argenson
(53.57.03.11)
MARKETS Wednesday, Saturday
FESTIVALS Easter Fair; November Fair of St Martin

HOTELS

Cyrano, 2 boul. Montaigne (53.57.02.76). Pleasant, small, old-style hotel with enclosed glass pavement terrace, known to generations of locals for good food. Now excellent. 'Modern-Périgourdine.' ROOMS D. MEALS C–F. Shut 26 June–19 July; 18–28 December; Sunday evening low season.

Bordeaux Hotel, Restaurant Le Terroir, 38 place Gambetta (53.57.12.83). Run by Maury family since 1855. Accommodation improved. Swimming-pool. Classical cooking, good-value meals. ROOMS D–E. MEALS B–E. Shut 20 December–1 February.

Flambée, route Périgueux 3km (53.57.52.33). Outstanding 'three-chimney' Logis de France with pretty country-style rooms, nice atmosphere and service and fine, traditional regional cooking. ROOMS D–F. MEALS A–D. Shut 2 January–20 March; Sunday evening, Monday low season.

Brive-la-Gaillarde

[MAP 3, page 198]

Though it is in Corrèze and is on the Corrèze river, Brive-la-Gaillarde is one of the essential link towns on the North Dordogne road system, at the meeting of N89, N20 and N121, as well as being a major rail junction on routes Paris–Toulouse and Bordeaux–Clermont–Ferrand. It is also a destination for motor-rail car-carrying trains from Boulogne (mid-May–mid-October), Paris and Lille (mid-May–mid-October). Although it has a big station and a vast, attractive station square with cafés and restaurants, it neither looks, nor is, a 'railway town', for it is an important centre for fruit-growing and market gardening.

The old town is surrounded by tree-lined boulevards where the ramparts used to be. These were so formidable that Brive earned the accolade of '*la Gaillarde*' (the Gallant) for the way it withstood sieges. It is a lively, outgoing town, without much of very special interest but never boring. Its Saturday market offers superb fruit, vegetables and regional specialities of Périgord. It is held outside the thirteenth-century church of St Martin, much restored over the centuries.

Some old houses have survived around the church, including the Renaissance Tour des Échevins. Two streets to the south-east is the magnificent Hôtel de Labenche, a beautiful old Renaissance mansion in near-golden stone. It is now used as a library and is not open to the public. But you can walk into the inner courtyard to see the graceful, big, rounded arcades under the wings of the house.

The Musée Ernest-Rupin, in a Louis XIII mansion in rue Dr Massenat, has been reorganized. Mostly it is of archeological interest, with some well-laid out prehistoric implements. A few simple medieval and Renaissance religious paintings are quite interesting, but of most interest to me is the collection of Empire furniture, Aubusson tapestries and memorabilia given by Lord Campbell, one of Napoleon's guards on Elba.

A local boy who succeeded, even if he did not really make

good, was Guillaume Dubois, born in 1656, the son of a poor apothecary. He rose to be tutor, then secretary to the Duc de Chartres, who became Duc d'Orléans and Regent of France in 1715 for the young King Louis XV. Dubois became very powerful in France. He was appointed Foreign Minister and Archbishop of Cambrai and made an alliance with England at the expense of Spain. He achieved his ambition of becoming a cardinal despite a debauched life, which he refused to give up undeterred by warnings from his doctor that he was killing himself. In 1722 he was made Prime Minister. Next year he died, true to form, in the arms of a lovely young woman.

A different sort of man was Guillaume Brune, born in Brive in 1763. He joined the army in 1791, and within seven years was a general commanding the Napoleonic troops in Italy. In 1799, he was appointed to command the French in Holland, and twice defeated the Duke of York, who previously had been so successful in this campaign. That was the Duke who 'marched his men to the top of the hill and marched them down again' in the satirical song. He became a symbol of the Revolution, but when he joined Napoleon again in 1815 he was murdered by Royalist opponents in Avignon.

Roads from Brive go through some lovely countryside. The N89 to Tulle has some attractive stretches beside the Corrèze river. The D38 to the interesting old town of Collonges-la-Rouge is beautiful, with several fine views over the Corrèze countryside.

TOURIST INFORMATION place 14 Juillet (55.24.08.80)
MARKETS Tuesday, Thursday, Saturday
FESTIVALS July–Festival de la Bourrée; early January–
Foie Gras and Truffle Fair; last Sunday in August–Melon
Fair; September–Walnut Fair; November–Book Fair

HOTELS

Crémaillère, 53 ave de Paris (55.74.32.47). Some of the best cooking I have found in a Logis de France. Old-style, straightforward, hearty meals, described locally as 'strong as the rugby team'. (Brive is very much rugby territory.) One menu 'follows the goose'. Tables in flower garden in summer. ROOMS D. MEALS D–F. Shut Sunday evening, Monday.

Truffe Noire, 22 boul. Anatole France (55.74.35.32). True regional cooking with the odd modern dish. ROOMS E–F. MEALS C–F. Open all year.

See also Varetz, page 187.

RESTAURANT

Périgourdine, 15 ave Alsace-Lorraine (55.24.26.55). Charming restaurant and garden. Good value. MEALS D–G. Shut 11–22 April; 15–29 July; Sunday.

Périgueux

[MAP 2, page 196]

Périgueux promises so much – in gastronomy, in history, in architecture. But you will never see it unless you park your car and walk. The traffic is fearsome. Many of the more modern buildings are a mess. But explore the old town, find the right restaurants and you will be splendidly rewarded. There's a big car-park in place Francheville where avenue Pompidou meets cours Fénelon.

The centre of the old town area is the huge, domed, ostentatious cathedral which seems to have strayed from old Constantinople. As you approach the town from the south, on the bridge over the river Isle, you can see five domes shining over the browny-red roofs of the houses and short minarets pointing skywards, all backed by a great square belltower topped by a stubby conical spire. Alas, as you get closer, St Front's

Périgueux

Cathedral looks more grandiose than beautiful and elegant. Last century, when it had become delapidated and really did need restoring, the local dignitaries refused to give the job to Viollet-le-Duc, who had restored Notre-Dame in Paris, and chose instead Abadie, who was later responsible for Sacré Coeur in

Paris. As a restorer, he was known by fellow-architects as 'The ·Wrecker'. He seemed determined to leave his mark on historic buildings in the grand manner. At Périgueux he rebuilt almost everything. He added seventeen turrets, scrapped a Romanesque refectory to give the cathedral a more geometric shape, and even replaced original Romanesque carvings with nineteenth-century work. Luckily, the Romanesque work was saved for Périgord Museum. Abadie based Sacré Coeur on his own version of Périgueux Cathedral. Thank goodness he was not around to be let loose on Reims after its Second World War damage!

The inside is grand but bare, like great stone wine cellars with all the wine drunk. The pillars are enormous, the domes high, and it is lit from chandeliers made last century in Byzantine style.

The church was consecrated in 1047 but burnt out in 1120 and only four bays of the original remain. The new one was built with five cupolas in the shape of a Greek cross, based on the former Church of the Apostles in Jerusalem. During the War of Religion in 1575, Protestants entered the town disguised as peasants going to the market, pillaged the church and took over the city. Over centuries the building became delapidated and was badly patched up.

St Front was not a cathedral until 1669. From the twelfth century until then the cathedral was the church of St Étienne-de-la-Cité. The restoration of St Étienne is nearly finished. It was built by St Front himself on the ruins of an old temple of Mars. He converted the Pagans to Christianity.

Tour de Vésone, 300 metres south of St Étienne, was the Gallo–Roman Cella or Holy of Holies – a temple 24 metres high and nearly as much in diameter. It was built in honour of the Goddess Vesunna, protector of the Petrocorii tribe, which gave its name to the town. Legend says that St Front threw out a demon from the pagan temple with such force that the demon went out through the wall, leaving a hole in the circle of the tower. Scholars say that this hole opens up to the rising sun for sun worship.

St Étienne Cathedral originally had a four-domed roof but the Protestants knocked down two of the domes and in the

Fronde uprising of aristocrats against the power of the king (1649–53) it was despoiled again. Close to it, but now in the centre of a large, busy square, are the remains of the first-century Roman arena, once holding 20,000 blood-lusting spectators watching lions, gladiators and Christian martyrs carved to pieces. It is now a park and children's playground, and it stands in a modern part of the city.

The St Front area around the present cathedral has steep, cobbled and narrow medieval streets where you meet few tourists, although it has lovely fifteenth- to sixteenth-century buildings with Renaissance turrets, staircases and balconies and delightful courtyards. You can find the best in rue de la Constitution (do look at No. 7, an eighteenth-century mansion that has an inner courtyard with spiral staircase and well), and rues Limogeanne, Miséricorde, Éguillerie and Nation. Some of the cobbled alleyways are particularly steep and rather dodgy underfoot, but it's worth the effort to explore them. Little streets around place de la Cloderc near the town hall north-west of the cathedral have nice cafés and restaurants, and in the *place* a little street market is held on weekday mornings. In place de la Clautre, where they used to execute people, the much larger market serving the surrounding countryside is held right alongside the cathedral on Wednesday and Saturday, and here you will find *foie gras*, truffles, *confits* and pâtés which are gastronomic proof that Périgueux is the capital of Périgord.

Do go down from the cathedral to the river Isle. Here beside the quays are the old houses of the fifteenth- and sixteenth-century merchants. Delightful and still lived in.

The most interesting items in the Périgord Museum, in a former monastery in Cours Tourny, are prehistoric finds from near Les Eyzies and Gallo-Roman mosaics (shut Tuesday). (*See also* Chancelade Abbey, page 105).

TOURIST INFORMATION Office de Tourism, 1 ave Aquitaine (53.53.10.63)
Department of Dordogne – CDT, 16 rue Président Wilson (53.53.44.35)
MARKETS Wednesday, Saturday (*see* text)

FESTIVALS July–August–International Mime Festival,
mid–30 September–Fair-Exposition

HOTELS

Périgord, 74 rue Victor-Hugo (53.53.33.63). Our old favourite.
Pleasant rooms. Real Perigordian dishes at reasonable prices.
Pretty courtyard and garden with tables. ROOMS B–D. MEALS
A–D. Shut 25 October–3 November; February holidays; Sunday
evening, Saturday.
Domino, 21 place Francheville (53.08.25.80). Fine old Relais de
Poste in town centre. Delightful courtyard for summer eating.
True Perigordian cooking, several menus. Spacious old-style
rooms. ROOMS B–F. MEALS B–G. Open all year.
Château de Rognac, at Bassilac, 7km E (53.54.40.78). Logis de
France in strange sixteenth-century château (*Monument Histori-
que*) on an island in river Isle. ROOMS C–E. MEALS C–F. Shut 1
November–15 March; Monday low season.

RESTAURANTS

Oison, 31 rue St Front (53.09.84.02). Régis Chiorozas offers
some of the best Perigordian cuisine you will find. Cheaper
menu superb value. MEALS D–G. Shut mid-February–early
March; 1–14 July; Sunday evening, Monday.
Flambée, 2 rue Montaigne (53.53.23.06). Reliable old restaurant
all locals know. In a sixteenth-century house. Classic regional
dishes. MEALS C–F. Shut 21 June–mid-July; Sunday.

Sarlat-la-Canéda

[MAP 2, page 197]

Though summer crowds are formidable and we cannot then be sure of a seat in our old favourite restaurant, our love for Sarlat is not diminished. Go in early May or autumn if you can, but *do* go. Blessedly, cars are banned from the very old centre of the town and I do not recommend driving along narrow streets and under the arches at any time. You would see little, anyway. Walk down small alleys and streets regardless of your map, and find hidden treasures.

Sarlat really was in decay when we found it after the Second World War. The only visitors we met were French and were serious scholars of medieval architecture. In a row of six lovely old houses, two might have been inhabited – but without many mod cons – two might still have been rescuable, but two would have been in complete decay. It was not suffering from war damage – just utter neglect. Not many French in those days had the same, almost sentimental, love of old buildings as the British have. Although they now believe in restoring old châteaux and big historic buildings, many French people have expressed wonderment to me that the British should buy and restore an old farm cottage when they could buy a nice, comfortable, modern bungalow. But an adopted son of Sarlat had plans to raise France's interest in the historic and architectural heritage of its provinces.

The historian and novelist André Malraux and his friend Josette Clotis moved to Sarlat just before the Second World War, entranced by its old streets and buildings. When war came, he joined the French army, was captured and imprisoned by the Germans. He escaped to the then-unoccupied Riviera, but in 1942 returned to the Dordogne to join the Resistance. He contacted other Resistance fighters locally and de Gaulle in London and became 'Colonel Berger', commanding the FFI Resistance Group covering Dordogne, Corrèze and Lot. He was wounded, captured and imprisoned in Toulouse.

After the war, de Gaulle made him first Minister of Propaganda and then, in 1958, Minister of Culture. He pushed through a law for the protection and restoration of buildings and old areas of towns. The law also mentioned Sarlat as an example. By the time he left the Ministry, six years later, the work of restoring Sarlat was progressing. Now the town is a treasure trove of medieval and Renaissance houses lining fine old streets. Some houses had to be pulled down, and during the demolition 350 coins were found bearing the effigy of England's Black Prince. Sarlat was an English garrison town for ten years from 1360.

Sarlat is no museum-town. It is a working commercial centre with good shops, restaurants and some good hotels, and it remains one of the most important in south-west France.

The Saturday market spreads over many streets and squares. In the old market place in the last weeks of July and the first in August classical drama is played by groups of visiting

Sarlat

actors, including a group from *Comédie Française*. Through the market you reach Marché des Oies, the historic goose market where you still see geese for sale, alive, dead and as *confit* in tins and jars, as well as chickens and all other manner of meat, fish, vegetables, cheese and fruit. The market spreads into place de la Liberté and along a stretch of the Traverse (rue de la République), a street driven, in the name of progress, right through the lovely old town in 1837 because local dignitaries thought that the horse-traffic had become intolerable!

All these market squares are surrounded by superb old houses. Round the corner from place du Marché des Oies in rue des Consuls is a beautiful fourteenth-century house, Hôtel Plamon, which belonged to a family of cloth merchants. The ground floor is like a courtyard with arcades used for selling or dyeing cloth. A fine staircase leads to the living rooms with restored Gothic windows. The water necessary for clothmaking came from the river Cuze which passes under it. In fact, except between rue des Consuls and the Traverse, it now passes under the town. There is a wonderful muddle of tiny medieval streets off rue des Consuls after it has crossed to the east side of the Traverse – a lovely area to explore. Along rue Jean-Jacques Rousseau is the twelfth-century Chapelle des Pénitents Blancs, where the poorer people of the town worshipped.

Place de la Liberté has many fine houses, especially a superb sixteenth-century mansion Hôtel de Maleville, which is now the Sarlat tourist office. It was made by joining three houses together; one façade is French Renaissance, another Italian Renaissance. It belonged to Jean Vienne, a Sarlat man who rose to high office under Henri IV after Henri's beautiful and astute mistress Gabrielle d'Estrées had befriended him. In gratitude he put Henri and Gabrielle's medallions each side of his door. He must have had a way with royal mistresses, for when Gabrielle died he became a favourite of her successor, Catherine de Balzac d'Entraygues.

Opposite is the imposing and pleasant Hôtel de Ville, built in 1618, recently well restored. Up rue Salamandre beside Hôtel de Ville, then left along rue du Présidial takes you past a number of lovely medieval and Renaissance buildings, including the impressive old Royal Seat of Justice (the *Présidial*), now a private house.

Place Liberté is overlooked by the forlorn tower of the former parish church of St Mary, which was started in 1365, finished in 1507, turned into an arms-store after the Revolution, then used by a baker, a coalman, as shops and as a post office. Now it is offices, and its 25-metre-high belltower has lost both its bells and the church pulpit from which St Bernard preached against the Albigensian heresy, and blessed bread brought to him, saying that if anyone ate it they would be cured of the plague.

Rue de la Liberté leads to the cathedral, with place de Peyrou at the west end. The large and beautifully restored mansion on the opposite corner is Hôtel de la Boétie, where Montaigne's friend Étienne de la Boétie was born in 1530. (In those days, of course, 'hôtel' meant mansion – not a hotel as we know it.) The house, built by his father in 1520, is Sarlat's finest Renaissance building and has a richly carved façade with delicate columns and tracery, and mullioned windows. La Boétie was a brilliant man, counsellor in the Bordeaux *parlement* at the age of twenty-four, poet, essayist and translator of Greek classics. He wrote 'Voluntary Servitude', an essay regarded as subversive in those days. It said that a tyrant gained power not from his own ability or strength but from the servitude of people who supported him to gain profit or position; those who did not rebel against tyranny were as guilty as the tyrants. He died at thirty-six and is remembered mostly for Montaigne's 'Essay on Friendship' which is about him.

The cathedral is dedicated to St Sacerdos, a monk who is supposed to have cured lepers and to have raised his father from the dead. He became Bishop of Sarlat and died in AD520. The church was originally built in the twelfth century and his bones transferred there. In 1273 the Abbot of the Monastery was shot in the church by an arrow fired by one of his own monks and the building had to be reconsecrated. The church became so dilapidated in the Hundred Years War that in the sixteenth century it was almost entirely rebuilt. The Romanesque belfry is from the earlier church, except the bulbous top, added in the eighteenth century. In the Wars of Religion, the Protestant leader, Geoffroi de Vivans, had the saint's bones cremated and thrown to the winds. A few bones were left, however, and are carried in procession round the town twice a year.

The old bishop's palace on the south side in place du Peyrou is now Sarlat's theatre. It is a superb Renaissance building, made for the Italian Cardinal Niccolo Gaddi, appointed Bishop of Sarlat in 1533. He brought Italian artists and workmen from the Medicis' court in Florence to decorate his palace. It has two storeys in stone, topped by one in delicate brick, with a polygon tower.

Beside the church is the Chapelle des Pénitents Bleus, where the richer citizens worshipped away from the poor. Between this and the cathedral is a garden made from the old cemetery, with some twelfth- to fifteenth-century tombstones still there. Steps at the end lead to a twelfth-century tower with a high, conical stone roof. It is something of a mystery. Some say that it was put up to commemorate St Bernard's miracle of the bread. Others say that it was a funeral chapel where bodies were kept awaiting burial or to await burning during the Plague.

Fifty metres from Chapelle des Pénitents is cours des Fontaines, with an ancient fountain which still works. Follow rue Tourny to rue J.–J. Escande to the huge place de la Grande Rigaudie with a crumbling statue of Étienne de la Boétie showing, perhaps, the indifference of the Sarlat people to their great, but underestimated, philosopher. The square is a useful car-park on weekdays. On Saturday another big market is held there. Sarlat has a market on Wednesday, too, at place Marché. The markets are quite outstanding, and still a wonderful show.

Alongside place Grande-Rigaudie are the Law Courts, and behind them the public gardens. They were laid out for Bishop François de Salignac and his nephew Fénelon in the seventeenth century by Le Nôtre, who planned Versailles gardens. Le Nôtre could not visit Sarlat, but sent his plan and his pupil Porchier to supervise the planting. Time has altered the gardens but they are still some of the most pleasant in the south-west, and from here you look down on the town over its ancient roofs and towers.

TOURIST INFORMATION place Liberté (53.59.27.67)
MARKETS Wednesday, Saturday (*see* text)
FESTIVALS July, August – theatre performances in place
Marché aux Oies

HOTELS

Madeleine, 1 place Petite Rigaudie (53.59.10.41). Still a favourite of Sarlat's regular visitors, serving true Perigordian dishes as it did thirty years ago on my first visit. Formal, old-fashioned, reliable. ROOMS E. MEALS C–G. Open 15 March–early September.

St-Albert et Montaigne, place Pasteur (53.59.01.09). Our old favourite; lively restaurant serving lovely Perigordian dishes with good portions in friendly, informal atmosphere. Good wines – Jean Jouffreau's superb old Cahors and Court-les-Mûts Bergerac. Posher bedrooms in Hôtel Montaigne opposite. ROOMS C–E. MEALS C–F. Shut Sunday evening, Monday in winter.

Hoirie, route Canéda, 2km S by D704 and C1 (53.59.05.62). Old hunting lodge of de Vienne family converted into hotel of character. Quiet. ROOMS E–G. MEALS E–G. Open 15 March–15 November.

Meysset, 3km NW by D6 Les Eyzies road (53.59.08.29). Fine old country mansion in large wooded grounds on hill overlooking two valleys. ROOMS E–F. MEALS B–F. Open end April–early October. Restaurant shut Wednesday lunch.

Couleuvrine, 1 place Bouquerie (53.59.27.80). Delightful, simple hotel built into thirteenth-century ramparts; charming little rooms. Huge fireplace in former guard room, now the restaurant. ROOMS C–E. MEALS C–E. Shut 15 November–1 December; 10 January–1 February.

RESTAURANT

Auberge de la Lanterne, 18 boul. Nesmann (53.59.05.54). Simple restaurant, rich Perigordian dishes. Wide range of menus.

MEALS B–F. Shut 1 January–1 March; Thursday evening, Friday.

Tulle

[MAP 3, page 198]

Tulle is squeezed between a narrow gorge of the Corrèze river and has had to expand in a snake along the banks, its main road following the river's twists and bends and its old houses rising in terraces up the hillsides. Although it has only 20,000 inhabitants, it is the capital of the Corrèze department and quite an important business and industrial centre.

However, it had a violent history until modern times. It grew up around an abbey believed to have been built on the site of a temple dedicated to the Roman goddess Tutela. The monks of Tulle were aggressive and had an eye for business. The monks of Marcilhac who controlled the Sanctuary at Rocamadour took little interest in it. The monks of Tulle installed themselves and when a body was discovered in 1166, which was claimed to be that of St Amadour, they cashed in, and the pilgrims came from far and wide. The Marcilhac monks then returned and threw them out. So the Abbot of Tulle appeared with a small army of monks and threw out the Marcilhac monks. Lawsuits followed, but even the Pope could not decide which monks should occupy Rocamadour. Finally the Abbot of Tulle bribed the Marcilhac monks to give up their claim and Tulle Abbey prospered on the proceeds of the pilgrimages.

Another Abbot of Tulle, Elie de Ventadour, found a different way to make money. He borrowed large sums at high rates of interest from Jewish bankers in Brive, who must have imagined that their capital was safe in the hands of such a pillar of the Roman Church. But the Abbot controlled the courts, and when he had the wealth stacked away in the Abbey, he had the bankers charged with usury, condemned and all their property confiscated.

Tulle Abbey came under the jurisdiction of Limoges Abbey, whose monks shared in Tulle's wealth until 1317, when the Abbot of Tulle got himself made Bishop of Tulle, and deprived Limoges of power over it. Lawsuits and arguments lasted so long that a touch of enmity between the towns survived into last century.

In the Hundred Years War, the English took the town twice, but the locals threw them out. In the Wars of Religion Tulle was on the Catholic side. The Protestant Viscount of Turenne failed to take it in 1577, but came back in 1585 and sacked it.

Two days after D-Day in 1944, the local Resistance rather prematurely threw out the Germans and declared Tulle to be liberated. The SS descended on it, hanged ninety-nine of the local people from their own balconies and deported hundreds more. A hundred and one never came back.

The fine silk net used for dresses and veils was originally made in Tulle and is still called after it.

It is not a very pretty town, but the old area north of the river (called Enclos) has steep winding streets with attractive medieval and Renaissance houses. Maison de Loyac is a fine fifteenth-century house with stone carvings round the door and windows, and there are others in rues Tour Maïsse, Porte Chanac and Porte Riche.

The cathedral's tall spire looks delightful from across the bridge. Built in the twelfth century, it was badly damaged in the eighteenth century when the transept and choir collapsed. The graceful belfry, 70 metres high, has two storeys of the twelfth and thirteenth centuries, capped with a granite spire originally of the fourteenth century. It was struck by lightning in the seventeenth century but an exact replica was built. A small museum adjoining the church has carvings in wood, firearms, Limoges porcelain and an interesting collection of old firebacks.

There is some fine scenery reached easily by roads or lanes from Tulle. The D23 north follows the right bank of the Corrèze through a narrow valley, then the Vimbelle valley to Vimbelle village. The N89 follows the river nearly all the way to

Brive. The little D7 north-west and the winding N120 south-east to Forgès are lovely, and the D940 goes through delightful country all the way to the Dordogne at Beaulieu-sur-Dordogne. The very attractive D53 east, off N89 north-east, leads to Gimel-les-Cascades (waterfalls, *see* page 119) and there is a nice but winding route back to Tulle by D26, D29, D978 and N120.

TOURIST INFORMATION quai Baluze (55.26.59.61)
Closed Monday, Sunday low season
MARKETS Daily covered market
FESTIVALS Easter–Antique Fair; 23 June – Pèlerinage
(Pilgrimage) de la Lunade

HOTELS

Toque Blanche, 29 rue Jean-Jaurès (55.26.75.41). Big, classic rooms and very good regional cooking. ROOMS B–C. MEALS C–F. Shut 1–30 January; Sunday low season.
Limouzi, 16 quai République (55.26.42.00). Town centre. Friendly. Bar-restaurant with excellent food. ROOMS C–D. MEALS B–E. Shut 1–8 January; Sunday except lunch in summer.

RESTAURANT

Central, 32 rue Jean-Jaurès (55.26.24.46). Lively, happy, often so crowded that you rub elbows. Brasserie also. MEALS C–E. Shut 22 July–13 August; Sunday evening, Saturday.

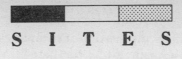

SITES

Les Eyzies Caves

[MAP 2, page 197]

I am not a cave-man and my knowledge of prehistory and
archaeology is negligible. However I do recommend that some-
time you spend two days and nights at the campsite or at one of
the hotels around the attractive little town of Les Eyzies-de-
Tayac, 21km north-west of Sarlat, to see the caves of our remote
ancestors. There is so much to see which is interesting and
enjoyable. And you need not spend all your time in caves and
museums, for it is a small resort, if a bit crowded until evening,
with a sailing and swimming centre, and a good choice of restaurants. These include two which offer pricey but really excellent meals – the Centenaire and the Cro-Magnon.

In 1868, men moving earth to build the Périgueux-to-Agen
railway uncovered, in a cave at a place called Cro-Magnon beside
the Vézère river, the skeletons of a man, woman and child.
Whether the Cro-Magnon family appreciated being disturbed in
their peaceful tomb after about 35,000 years is doubtful, but
their discovery led to a harvest of archaeological finds in the
valley – so many that the little town has long been called the
Capital of Prehistory.

Five years before the Cro-Magnon family was found, two
now-famous archaeological researchers, Édouard Lartet and
Henry Christy, had uncovered, close by at La Madeleine, a
carved and chiselled mammoth tusk. The discoveries which followed gave us invaluable knowledge of our ancestors.

It appears that herds of reindeer were driven south by the
Second Ice Age and men who lived by hunting them followed.
The Vézère river was a perfect place to settle, with convenient

caves and rock shelters. At the time, the river was much higher, coming well up cliffs which now tower up to 80 metres above it.

As well as visiting the caves do go to the castle of the former Barons of Beynac, built in the eleventh and twelfth centuries beneath an overhanging rock, and restored in the sixteenth century. Although the statue of Primitive Man by Dardé on the platform seems to be of man born considerably before Cro-Magnon man, inside is the Musée National de Préhistoire, set up by Denis Peyrony and presented to the nation. It is most interesting and instructive (shut Tuesday). You will not see it all. Some exhibits are reserved for international archaeologists and other scholars. But there is plenty to keep me happy.

Fairly early in the morning, before you go to the caves, try to book tickets for the guided tours. Groups are limited to avoid damage. (At Grotte de Font-de-Gaume, the notice says that groups are limited to twenty people. There used to be another notice stating also that reductions were given to groups of over twenty-five!) You can get information about caves and opening times from the Syndicat d'Initiative, place Mairie (tel. 53.06.97.05). Open from 15 March to 31 October.

To laymen, the most interesting cave is Grotte de Font-de-Gaume, 500 metres from Les Eyzies. It is 120 metres long, with side-chambers, and has been known for centuries. It has more than 200 wall paintings of mammoths, bison, horses, reindeer and other deer, including a superb frieze of dark-brown bison on a white limestone background. They were painted about 40,000 years ago and the reaction of most people is to wonder *why* they were painted. Experts in many fields have had their say. For a long time, the theory of the Abbé Henri Breuil, a great expert on prehistoric art, was believed by most people. He thought it was a form of primitive religion or magic. Men painted animals to ensure plentiful game, that they would breed and increase. Human figures on cave walls were sorcerers, making magic, he said. Today that theory is not entirely believed. More and more people now think that this was the blossoming of art – that our ancestors were decorating their caves for pleasure. Many of the cave drawings show great realism and even beauty (guided tours of cave – 1 April to September, shut Tuesday; 1 to 11 November, 25 November to 25 December).

Grotte des Combarelles (3km along D47 east of Les Eyzies) has two caves, discovered in 1901. One, with a long winding passage, has drawings of 300 animals, including mammoths shown resting and running. A second has cave drawings and signs of habitation, including tools and traces of domestic middens (guided tours – ten people only, shut Tuesday; 25 November to 25 December).

Gisement de Laugerie Haute (north-west of Les Eyzies to left of D47), is an attractive spot at the foot of high cliffs where diggings since 1863 have revealed work and art of cavemen over thousands of years (guided tours – shut Tuesday; 25 November to 25 December).

Basse Laugerie (just before Haute Laugerie on D47) has a good display of tools, weapons and bones found under loose stones (open Easter to 30 September).

Grotte de St Cirq (south-west of Les Eyzies off D706) has a human figure as well as animal drawings.

In Gorges d'Enfer (north-west of Les Eyzies, just off D47) is a small valley with a reserve where animals portrayed in the caves (tigers, bison, red deer, fallow deer, moufflons, wild boar and horses) can be seen in semi-liberty from forest trails (open mid-March to mid-November).

La Roque St Christophe, a 500-metre-long vertical cliff rising 80 metres above the Vézère river, looks like a massive honeycomb. The hundreds of holes in it are caves, hollowed out on five tiers. Prehistoric man used these caves. Traces of art and tools (now in the Eyzies National Museum) were found there. But later, in the tenth century, they were made into a fortress where the local people held out against the Norsemen who rowed their ships right up these rivers each spring to loot, burn, rape and kill, leaving a destitute countryside behind them in winter when they went home with loot and prisoners. The caves were used again as a defence and hideout against marauding bands of soldiers and robbers in the Hundred Years War. The fortress was destroyed in the Wars of Religion, but the stepped pathway cut to the caves is still there. It is called Pas de Miroir because the Vézère used to flow much higher up the cliff and you could see your reflection in the water. From the terrace you can look down on the whole valley (guided tours in season).

The twelfth-century fortified church by the railway station has crenellated belfries for defence.

TOURIST INFORMATION Syndicat d'Initiative, place Mairie (mid-March–October – 53.06.97.05)
MARKET Monday

HOTELS

Centenaire (53.06.97.18). Charming, comfortable, with superb cooking by Roland Mazère, one of the best chefs in France. Perigordian dishes, many old and traditional, with his own variations. Expensive, but well worth it. Swimming-pool. ROOMS E–G. MEALS F–G. Shut early November–end March; Tuesday lunch.

Cro-Magnon, route de Périgueux (53.06.97.06). Pleasant garden with shady terrace. Very good cooking with a strong Perigordian accent. Swimming-pool. ROOMS E–F. MEALS D–G. Shut 15 October–15 April. Restaurant shut Wednesday lunch.

Glycines (53.06.97.07). Lovely house with antique furniture in a big garden by the river. Nice terrace; pool. Modern cooking of true regional ingredients. ROOMS E. MEALS C–G. Shut 1 November–15 April; Saturday lunch.

Centre, place Mairie (53.06.97.13). Friendly, comfortable Logis de France in typical old Périgord house in town centre; garden with river walk. Six good-value regional menus. ROOMS C–D. MEALS A–G. Open end March–15 November.

Grotte de Lascaux

[MAP 2, page 197]

Lascaux Cave, near the small town of Montignac on the Vézère river (*see* page 144), is one of the greatest prehistoric finds in Europe and one of the most interesting. I count myself very lucky to have been inside before it had to be closed to the public, in 1963. After the magnificent wall paintings had survived for 17,000 years, visitors introduced bacteria, algae and carbon monoxide from their breath which threatened to destroy them. But Lascaux is still worth visiting, for in a disused quarry 250 metres from the original cave is Lascaux II. With the help of stereoscopic picures and computers, the painter Monique Peyrac has reproduced brilliantly the two most important galleries of the cave – the Bull chamber, showing a remarkable great charging black bull, and the Painted Gallery. This reproduction of the cave includes a very interesting museum showing the story of the cave, which was occupied about 15,000 years BC.

In the cave are engravings of bison pierced by arrows, herds of deer, prancing horses, an animal hauntingly like a unicorn, and the bull. One figure has a man's body and a bird's head.

The colours were so remarkably clear when the cave was found in 1940 that the drawings were called fakes by some experts. Now it has been established, as far as science can tell, that they are authentic and that they were protected from moisture and the formation of stalactites by an impermeable layer of fine-grained chalk on the ceiling and a layer of carbonate of lime on the walls.

Some drawings are superimposed on others, suggesting that they were made through several generations. Unlike many caves, discovered and then forgotten, the cave seems to have remained undiscovered for thousands of years. In the 1920s, a tree blew down and revealed an entrance, but there are so many caves and pot-holes in the Vézère valley that no one took much notice. It was called '*Le Trou du Diable*' (the Devil's Cave), so perhaps local people thought it prudent to stay away. Then, in 1940, five schoolboys looking for a secret 'gang' hide-out decided that it would do nicely. They explored further than most people and when they saw the splendid coloured drawings on the wall they were so overcome that they looked at them until their torch batteries ran out. But it was their secret and they told nobody until one day one of them mentioned the drawings to their school headmaster. He made them reveal their secret cave. The news spread quickly to the French archaeologist Abbé Breuil and so to the world.

The drawings were made, it seems, by mixing mineral-based pigments with animal fat which was then allowed to evaporate through hollow bones. The resultant coloured powder was then blown on to the walls. The bones and hollow vegetable blow pipes were found in the cave. So was a lamp made from a hollowed flint in which grease was placed with moss as a wick.

Theories suggest that the cave was a temple of primitive rites or a place of magic cults, but it seems as likely that it was the home of people who liked their walls beautifully decorated.

In midsummer there are often long queues for Lascaux II.

INFORMATION and HOTELS *See* Montignac, page 144.

Rocamadour

[MAP 2, page 197]

The spectacular little town of Rocamadour, clamped to a 150-metre rock face, grew from a hermit's cave to become one of the greatest sites of Christian pilgrimage and one of France's most lucrative tourist centres.

See it from the top terrace at l'Hospitalet, preferably when the morning sun is on the rocks, or lit up at night when it turns

into a fairy city, and you will never forget it. You look down on
its outline from the castle ramparts at the top of churches,
hotels, shops and houses to the gorge below the town, where the
river Alzou winds through fields. The main road of Rocamadour, packed with people and lined with souvenir shops, ice-
cream parlours, boutiques, cafés and restaurants all aimed at
relieving visitors of their money, is still high above the river.

It all started when a mystery hermit built an oratory in the
rock. When he died they called him Amadour and set up a
chapel. In 1166, a local man asked to be buried beneath the
chapel threshold. When the grave was dug they found the bones
of a man. They were placed near the chapel alter and immediately miracles began to happen and the hermit was canonized as
St Amadour.

Pilgrims came from all over Europe and made the town rich.
Many pilgrim penitents used to climb the 216 steps to the chapel
on their knees and in chains to plead forgiveness for their sins.
They would kneel before the altar while the priest recited
prayers and removed the chains. The priest gave each penitent a
certificate and a lead image of the Virgin. Many needed the
certificate as proof of their pilgrimage, for they had been sentenced to make it by the all-powerful Ecclesiastical Court. Pilgrims were a mixed bunch, from thieves and murderers to kings
and powerful rulers.

The town was fortified, but it was so rich that it was ransacked in the Hundred Years War by English and French
soldiers as well as the private armies of the freelance French
barons. In revolt against his father, Henry II of England's eldest
son, Henry Courtmantel, plundered the church treasure to pay
his army in 1183 and died of a sudden illness which he believed
to be sent by God as a punishment. The Protestant captain
Bessonies took Rocamadour during the Wars of Religion, dese-
crated the shrine and destroyed much of the town. The abbey
attached to it remained empty until the Revolution, when it was
shut down completely.

In the last century, an astute Bishop of Cahors had the
churches restored and revived the pilgrimages. Modern pilgrims don't go up on their knees, but a few bow the knee on
every step. They make for the tiny place St Amadour (le Parvis

Rocamadour

des Églises) where seven churches are squeezed in, including Chapelle Miraculeuse, the Chapel of Our Lady, where the hermit hollowed out his oratory. A new chapel was built last century. A rock fell on the old one.

In the main street are two of the thirteenth-century town gates and the town hall made from a restored fifteenth-century Maison des Frères of the abbey. Now it contains some superb tapestries of Causse flora and fauna by the great Jean Lurçat, who lived in Lot in an old castle at St Céré until his death in 1966.

TOURIST INFORMATION La Mairie (Easter–
15 November – 65.33.62.59)
FESTIVAL Easter–15 October – *son et lumière* nightly

HOTELS

Ste Marie (65.33.63.07). Perched on a rock face with small terrace; lovely views. Six menus. ROOMS B–D. MEALS A–G. Open 1 April–1 November.

Beau Site et Jehan de Valon Restaurant (65.33.63.08). Old house in town centre, lovely valley views. Fine old furnishings. Excellent modern regional cooking. ROOMS D–F. MEALS A–F. Open 1 April–12 November.

Vielles Tours, 2km W by D673 at Lafage (65.33.68.01). Country hideaway in restored manor, part thirteenth century. Logis de France. Regional cooking. Restaurant shut for lunch except weekends. ROOMS C–F. MEALS B–D. Shut early November–early April.

Château de Roumégouse, near Rignac, 4km SE just off N140 (65.33.63.81). Gorgeous neo-Gothic 'fairy-tale' château above Causse de Gramat. Resistance hide-out in Second World War. Lovely views. Charming. Regional dishes. Relais et Châteaux hotel. ROOMS E–G. MEALS E–G. Shut 31 October–15 April; restaurant shut Tuesday except evening in midsummer.

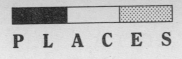

ABJAT-SUR-BANDIAT
[DORDOGNE]

Village with several old manor houses and castles around, it lies on the Bandiat river NE of Nontron, close to the Limousin border. In the lake under the shadow of the sixteenth-century Château Balleran you can fish, swim, paddle canoes or pedal pedaloes. There is a campsite nearby. Château de la Malignie is a formidable medieval fortress, but it is private property and not open to visitors. The Romanesque church with a big old bell-tower was built in the thirteenth century, modified later.

MARKET Last Tuesday of each month

AGONAC
[DORDOGNE]

This pleasant small market town in hilly country rich in walnut trees and truffle oaks is right off the tourist beat, 15km N of Périgueux by the D3. It is on the Beauronne river. The severe-looking fortified St Martin's church isolated in the nearby valley has a charming, interesting interior with Romanesque eleventh-century arched nave and twelfth-century cupolas. At the bottom of the main dome is a defence corridor with a field of fire (presumably for archers!) covering both sides of the choir. There is another defence chamber at openings in the belfry. The keep in the village was built in the twelfth century as an addition to the château, built by a bishop 200 years earlier to keep out the invading Norsemen. In the fifteenth century the present manor house was added.

MARKET Sunday

L'AIGLE BARRAGE
[CORRÈZE]

Middle of five dams for hydro-electric power on Upper Dordogne (*see* Argentat, page 73), making a lake with indented shoreline. You can see how impressive it is by leaving your car and walking on the D16 to the belvedere below it.

AJAT
[DORDOGNE]

This tiny hamlet 9km NW of Thénon (*see* page 174) and just N of the N89 has a fine Romanesque church and château which make an interesting group. The church, probably built in the twelfth century, has lost its two domes but has two square bays and a multi-sided apse, topped by what architects call an 'oven-vault' and stone slates. The château, built in the sixteenth century, is like two separate buildings joined by a gallery. Its walls are topped by battlements. Bauzens church (3km) is a really beautiful Romanesque building.

ALLASSAC
[CORRÈZE]

In the hilly country near to the Vézère river, north of Brive, this is a charming town which has old houses with slate roofs, an impressive keep called Caesar's Tower in drystone (left from the twelfth-century fortifications) and an unusual Gothic church built of black schist set off in places with red sandstone. It has a machicolated porch for greeting intruders with stones or boiling oil.

   This part of the countryside near the Vézère gorges is little known to tourists and a pleasant place for a peaceful stay – in the Logis de France at Allassac, at Donzenac, 6km SE, or at Colette's old château at Varetz (*see* page 187).
MARKET Daily

HOTEL

Midi, 14 ave Victor-Hugo (55.84.90.35). Simple Logis; cheap. ROOMS B–C. MEALS A–C. Shut 20 December–15 January.

ANNESSE-ET-BEAULIEU
[DORDOGNE]

14km W of Périgueux, near the river Isle, and N of the N89, it has fine old houses nearby and, on a rock above it, Château de Puy-St-Astier, built in the fifteenth to seventeenth centuries. The Romanesque church has a carved altar and statue of the Crucifixion. At Beaulieu, nearer to Périgueux, is the Château de Laroche Beaulieu, which now belongs to the Pasteur Institute.

HOTEL

Château de Lalande, across river Isle, reached through Razac, 3km NE. Château marked on yellow Michelin map for the area (53.54.52.30). ROOMS C–E. MEALS C–G. Open 15 March–15 November. Restaurant shut Wednesday low season.

ANTONNE-ET-TRIGONANT
[DORDOGNE]

Château country, 11km E of Périgueux on D705. Château des Bories, finished in 1604 and well restored in 1910, is a small manor house on a terrace above the river Isle, started in 1497 for Jeanne de Hautefort. Although it was intended to be fortified, its Renaissance windows add a touch of domesticity, as does the beautiful staircase inside the square tower, with a Gothic chapel on the ground floor and a little rest-room on each storey. The staircase leads to the eight bedrooms and was so admired that it was copied in several châteaux. Jeanne and her friends must have been gastronomes or gourmands. Despite the small size of the château, its kitchen is said to have the largest fireplace in the Dordogne, and attractive vaulted cellars.

You reach the château by a long avenue of trees. It has two round towers flanking the main building and the massive square battlement tower. It looks peaceful now, with rushes and wild flowers in the moat and a finely landscaped and attractive entrance from the river. It is privately owned and must be a very nice place to live. You can go inside to see the beautiful decorations, the Louis XIII furnishings in the great hall and the Flemish tapestry in shades of green in July and August.

Nearby are the fifteenth-century Château de Trigonant and the Château Lammary, also fifteenth century, altered in the eighteenth century. Château d'Escoire is surprisingly austere for a house built in the eighteenth century, though its main façade is decorated by a semi-circular rotunda, with attractive windows.

HOTEL

Hostellerie La Charmille, at Laurière (53.06.00.45). ROOMS C–E. MEALS B–G.

ARGENTAT
[CORRÈZE]

Argentat is a true gem – a beautiful, peaceful old town on both banks of the Dordogne river, where it breaks out of the rocky gorges into a delightful broader valley. Approach it from the south, where upstream from the bridge old stone houses come right to the water's edge, with overhanging wooden balconies and terraced gardens. From the bridge you can see the spires, turrets, slate roofs and rough stone of the houses on the far bank reflected in the fast-flowing river. The neat houses with pretty chestnut balconies and grey-tiled roofs line a wide quayside where 120 years ago flat-bottomed barges called *gabares* or *argentats* were built.

Argentat had the largest boat-building yards on the river upstream from Bergerac. The biggest boats had sails and carried passengers as well as wine and later coal. Some cargoes were shipped to new boats at Souillac but most went to Libourne, where the smaller *gabares*, made of oak, were broken up for their timber. The journey was dangerous, especially much further downstream at Lalinde. The very worst journey was for small boats passing through the gorges upstream to reach Argentat. Downstream the river runs more quietly in a wider valley through wooded hills, with sheep feeding in grass clearings, reaching Beaulieu after 25km.

There was no bridge across the Dordogne at Argentat until 1829, when the Comte de Noailles was allowed to build a wire bridge to bring coal from his small mine nearby. In the late seventeenth century it took the Princesse de Condé a whole day to ferry her household across the river.

2 km upstream from Argentat is Le Sablier dam, the last of the five great dams built to harness the wild upper waters of the Dordogne river to provide five per cent of France's hydro-electric power, which was finished in 1958. The others, going upstream, are Barrage de Chastang, l'Aigle Marèges (the only one built before the Second World War), and the great Bort-les-Orgues dam right on the Auvergne border. Argentat's dam can empty 880,000 gallons of water a second. It rises to a height of 35 metres.

The fourteenth-century square-towered Château de Gibanel is reflected in the river nearby. Argentat is a centre for canoeing, sailing and windsurfing, and an excellent quiet centre for extremely dramatic scenery.

TOURIST INFORMATION ave Pasteur (15 June–15 September – 55.28.16.05) or Mairie (rest of year – 55.28.10.91)

MARKET First and third Thursday of each month – market fair

HOTELS

Gilbert, rue Vachel (55.28.01.62). Logis de France. ROOMS C–F. MEALS A–F. Shut 15 December–15 March; Friday evening, Saturday in winter.

Fouillade, place Gambetta (55.28.10.17). Another Logis. ROOMS B–C. MEALS A–D. Shut early November–early December. Restaurant shut Monday in winter.

ARNAC
[See Château Pompadour, page 150]

ATUR
[Dordogne]

Village 13km S of Périgueux which has a twelfth-century Lanterne des Morts (Tower of the Dead), smaller than the one in Sarlat but equally puzzling. It is pierced by four rectangular openings. The church, part Romanesque, with an octagonal dome topped by a belfry, is unusual and handsome.

AUBAS
[Dordogne]

W of Montignac by the Vézère, Aubas has three châteaux. Château de Sauveboeuf by the river was knocked down by Richelieu in 1633 and rebuilt in Louis XIII style in a U-shape. The central building, with lovely dormer windows, is joined by two high wings. But one of its ornamental fountains is now in America, the other at Château de Clairvac in Lot. It belonged, in the eighteenth century, to the Counts of Mirabeau. Other châteaux nearby are La Fleurie (sixteenth to seventeenth century) and La Petite-Filoli (seventeenth century). The village church with eleventh-century capitals has a coloured carving of the Holy Family behind the altar.

AUBAZINE
[Corrèze]

In lovely countryside of wooded hills just S of the N89, 14km E of Brive, this village clusters round the old abbey church founded by St Étienne d'Aubazines (St Stephen) in the twelfth

century. You reach it on a little right turn off the N89 across a
bridge over the Corrèze river.

Stephen set up a hermitage, then founded an abbey which
soon prospered. The church is in pure Cistercian style, simple
outside and in. It lost six bays in the eighteenth century. The
simplicity makes the tomb of Stephen look really magnificent. It
is richly decorated with beautiful carvings of the saint and his
monks and nuns being greeted by Mary and Jesus on earth and
on the day of their resurrection. The choir stalls are decorated
with carved faces with many different expressions.

The former monastery buildings are now an orphanage run
by nuns. Stephen set up a convent for nuns in the nearby gorges
of the Coiroux river, a tributary of the Corrèze.

North of the village (3½km) is Puy de Pauliac, a hill with a
fine all-round view of the Corrèze valley.

HOTELS

Tour, place l'Église (55.25.71.17). Quiet Logis. ROOMS B–D.
MEALS A–E. Shut February; Monday lunch, Sunday low season.
Saut de la Bergère, 2km E by D48 (55.25.74.09). Tranquil Logis in
country with lake and golf-course nearby. ROOMS B–C. MEALS
B–E. Shut 1 December–28 February.
St-Étienne, place l'Église (55.25.71.01). Attractive; in old priory.
Regional dishes. ROOMS A–D. MEALS B–D. Open 1 March–
20 September.

AUDRIX
[DORDOGNE]

Over the Vézère river-bridge from Le Bugue a little road, the
D31F, takes you to the chasm of Proumeyssac and the pretty
town of Audrix, which is on a 200-metre peak giving excellent
views over the valleys of the Vézère and Dordogne. They meet
to the west.

A tunnel drilled into a hill just north takes you to a platform
built up the Proumeyssac chasm. You can see the whole dome of
the cavern with its strangely shaped stalactites, cleverly lit (open

daily Palm Sunday–30 September; Sunday in October). You can combine it with a visit to Bara-Bahau cave across the river (*see* Le Bugue, page 94).

AURIAC-DU-PÉRIGORD
[DORDOGNE]

5km N of Montignac, this village is built in the shadow of its castle, Château de la Faye, and was a place of pilgrimage in the Middle Ages. The château is really a group of buildings with a twelfth-century keep, fourteenth-century detached living quarters and towers of the fifteenth to sixteenth century. It includes Chapelle St Rémy, built in 1465 by Antoine de la Cropte, lord of the castle. It has delicate vaulted ogival arches.

St Rémy was a healing saint and pilgrims would take a little statue of him from its niche in the church and rub it over their infected parts, which would hardly have made it medically sanitary. In contrast to the chapel, the village church is heavily fortified.

AZERAT
[DORDOGNE]

Attractive little town 36km E of Périgueux on the Brive road and only 2km from La Bachellerie and Château de Rastignac (*see* La Bachellerie, page 77). Built in a square like a bastide, Azerat has very attractive houses from the Middle Ages to the eighteenth century and a town hall which was once a small château. Its Gothic Chapelle Notre-Dame-Espérance (Our Lady of Good Hope) was, in the Middle Ages, a pilgrimage church for sick children. The arms of the La Rochefoucauld family can be seen in the chapel. (Their former château was burned down in 1903.) François, the sixth Duc de La Rochefoucauld (1613–80), was a writer who became involved in so many love adventures and political intrigues against Richelieu and Mazarin that he had to live in exile for three years. When his *Mémoires* were published they caused such a scandal that he pretended that he had not written them. His final mistress was the novelist the Countess of La Fayette who wrote *La Princesse de Clèves*, a vivid picture of French court life.

LA BACHELLERIE
[DORDOGNE]

Small town on the D65 just before it reaches the N89. The church stands in ruins beside the river Cern, just as the English left it in the fourteenth century. On the N89 is the beautiful white Château de Rastignac, built between 1812 and 1817 by a local architect, Mathurin Blanchard, for the Marquis de Rastignac. It is a long building with a raised terrace in front and a beautiful semi-circular peristyle of Ionic columns, like a little temple, in the centre. It is uncommonly like the White House in Washington, DC, but 50 metres shorter, and many believe that the White House was copied from it. (That was probably why the Nazis set fire to it in 1945 – one of thousands of lovely buildings they destroyed in childish vandalism when they knew that they had lost the war.) It is in Palladian style, which was back in fashion at the time that it was built. Many buildings were going up all over Europe based on the style of the great Palladio.

Rastignac has been completely restored. You cannot visit it, but you can drive down the tree-lined avenue leading to it to get a better view.

BADEFOLS D'ANS
[DORDOGNE]

A pretty, tiny market town just S of Hautefort among a network of attractive little roads and hamlets that few tourists have penetrated. It is old-style Périgord farming country, well worth exploring – slowly. Small inns used by locals serve old-style country meals with huge portions at truly bargain prices. This is the old Pays d'Ans. In the fourteenth century a daughter of the Lord of Château de Hautefort married a Lord of Ans in Flanders and the lands around here were part of her dowry, so her new name was added to that of the villages.

The fifteenth-century château, which was altered a little in the eighteenth century to make it more comfortable to live in, was burned by the Germans in 1944, but the strong walls withstood the fire and it has been well restored. It is a true fortress on a hilltop, with machicolated walls and keep, dominating the countryside, but it is not open to visitors. There are good views from the village, which has a twelfth-century domed church with an eighteenth-century belfry.

MARKET Third Monday of each month – market fair

HOTEL
Tilleuls (53.51.50.08). Pretty little inn opposite château. Typical of the great-value inns around here, used by locals. Simple rooms. Garden with vines, trees and tables. ROOMS A–B. MEALS A. Shut Saturday low season.

BADEFOLS-SUR-DORDOGNE
[DORDOGNE]

On the left bank of the Dordogne river, just downstream from the spectacular Cingle de Trémolat loop, 25km E of Bergerac. Its ruined château on a cliff is still photogenic. Built in the twelfth and fifteenth centuries, it controlled the river in the days of barge-traffic and was the lair of robber-barons who stopped and looted the barges as they sailed downstream. It was destroyed during the Revolution, which must have given the local people much pleasure. The man who ordered its destruction was Joseph Lakanal, sent to govern the province of Bergerac.

There is good fishing here in the Dordogne, and also bathing at some times of the year. This is an attractive stretch of river, too, and there is a pleasant road to Cadouin. You meet few visitors in the attractive lanes to the south.

HOTEL
Lou Cantou (53.22.50.36). Good Perigordian cooking. ROOMS
B–C. MEALS C–F. Shut 1 November–1 April.

BANNES, CHÂTEAU
[DORDOGNE]

Elegant castle on a rocky spur dominating the Couze river valley
5km NW of Beaumont-du-Périgord (*see* page 81) and near the
D660 Bergerac road. It was built for a Bishop of Sarlat, Armand
de Gontaut Biron, around 1500 on the site of a castle destroyed
by the English. It is flanked with powerful round towers with
pepper-pot roofs and has a sentry walk, showing that the Bishop
was well prepared for an attack. It is approached across a drawbridge over a now-dry moat.

BARDOU
[DORDOGNE]

Village 7km E of Issigeac (SW Dordogne) which has a twelfth-
century church with a belltower rising from over the doorway.
The very interesting château was built in the fifteenth to seventeenth centuries and restored recently. It stands in a fine park.

BEAULIEU-SUR-DORDOGNE
[CORRÈZE]

Around AD855, Raoul the Archbishop of Bourges visited a place
on the Dordogne river called Vellinus by the Romans, changed
its name to 'Beau Lieu', the beautiful place, and founded a
Cluniac monastery there. It well deserves the name for its lovely
setting. It has such a warm and relaxed atmosphere that it has
been called the Limousin Riviera.

The monastery became so famous that at the start of the twelfth century the monks began the Romanesque abbey church of St Pierre, around which the town grew in the narrow streets which are still its centre. The church was built by masons of the School of Toulouse, who also worked at Carennac, Moissac and Souillac. They have left us some superb carving, especially the elaborate south porch. The semi-circle of its tympanum is crowned with the Last Judgement. Below are two rows of winged beasts and strange monsters. The church is large and imposing with a series of finely proportioned apses and a strong octagonal tower with a slate-covered spire. The treasure room has an elaborate twelfth-century Virgin in silvered wood and an enamelled thirteenth-century shrine. Here in the church the Napoleonic hero, Marshal Ney, the man who protected Napoleon's rearguard during the retreat from Moscow and led the centre at Waterloo, hid after Waterloo but was caught and shot for treason. The reason was that, after Napoleon's defeat at Leipzig and banishment to Elba, Ney joined the new King Louis XVIII and accepted great honours. When Napoleon escaped from Elba and was marching back to Paris, Ney was sent with an army to fight him but switched sides with his troops and made Napoleon's return possible.

There is a charming chapel with a twelfth-century belfry mirrored in the Dordogne river.

The monks of the monastery became lax and broke their vows, then abandoned the abbey in the Wars of Religion. It was reformed by the Benedictine Maurists but closed after the Revolution.

The D12 from Argentat is a lovely road and the busier D940 is attractive all the way to Tulle. 12km S of Beaulieu, just past Bretenoux, the river Cère meets the Dordogne.

TOURIST INFORMATION Syndicat d'Initiative, place Marbot (Easter–September – 55.91.09.94)

MARKET Saturday

FESTIVALS July, August – music concerts; August – Fête du Monturu; early September – Fête des Saints

HOTELS

Turenne, 1 boul. St-Rodolphe-de-Turenne (55.91.10.16). Full of character. In old town near the church. Large rooms with period furniture. ROOMS C–D. MEALS C–E. Shut 1 January– early February; Sunday evening, Monday, Tuesday lunch low season.

Central Fournié, 4 place Champ-de-Mars (55.91.01.34). Very attractive, in a lovely position on the river bank. Terrace and garden. ROOMS C–E. MEALS B–F. Open 15 March– 15 November.

BEAUMONT-DU-PÉRIGORD
[DORDOGNE]

A bastide founded in 1272 by the Seneschal of Guyenne for Edward I of England, which still has the original church, the ruins of its ramparts, many ancient arcaded houses and a superb fortified gate, Porte de Luzier, with a beautiful seventeenth-century mansion, Château de Luzier, alongside. You can see that invaders getting through the gate would have to have run down a narrow passage leading to more fortifications.

As with many bastides, the church was heavily fortified as a last defence if the enemy got past the fortified walls. It has four corner towers and a sentry walk, and the walls are bare apart from a beautiful but puzzling finely carved gallery above the porch, showing four evangelists, Edward I and a stag hunt.

Beaumont is an attractive town with two old-style inns and a fine arcaded market square where a fair is held monthly (*see* below). It is only 29km SE of Bergerac, and on the D660, but not many visitors have reason to come this way, except to reach the lovely bastide of Monpazier, and the roads around here are very attractive, especially the D660 to the Dordogne river, and the D26 towards Belvès. Château Bannes (*see* page 79) is 5km NW just off the D660.

TOURIST INFORMATION Mairie (Easter–September – 53.22.39.12)

MARKET Second Tuesday of each month – market fair

HOTELS

Voyageurs 'Chez Popaul' (53.22.30.11). Known for enormous help-yourself hors-d'œuvres table of forty-five items, big portions and its very pricey gastronomic menu. Completely renovated. ROOMS A–D. MEALS A–G. Shut January, February, October, November; Monday except July, August.

BEAUSSAC
[DORDOGNE]

An off-track village between Mareuil and Nontron in the unknown NW of Dordogne, it has a twelfth-century church and three Renaissance châteaux – de Bretanges (fifteenth to seventeenth centuries), d'Aucors and de Pontignac. Bretanges belonged to Alain de Moneys who made himself so unpopular with his peasants that, in the revolt of 1871, they assassinated and burned him.

BELVÈS
[DORDOGNE]

A lovely medieval town N of Monpazier in a spectacular hilltop setting above the river Nauze valley, with superb views. Arrive from the D710 and you can see the whole town – turrets and belltowers of the old houses, their terraced gardens and shrubberies. You come suddenly into place des Armes, which is lined with old shops, a fifteenth-century covered market and a chain attached to a pillar where poor wretches were flogged or pilloried for minor crimes. Climbing between new shops mixed with Gothic and Renaissance buildings, you reach place de la Croix des Frères, where there is an old Dominican monastery with an octagonal clock tower. Opposite is a true old inn. The ring road follows the old walls of the town, built around a château with a square twelfth-century tower. There are splendid views from the road over those old houses, towers and gardens

to the countryside beyond. This is walnut country and sales are held in season at the Saturday market in the old market square.
MARKET Saturday

BERBIGUIÈRES
[DORDOGNE]

A very attractive hamlet S of the Dordogne river on the lovely D50 road a few kms W of Beynac and Castelnaud. A small road crosses the river to St Cyprien 3km N. Berbiguières is built around a seventeenth-century château hiding behind its old walls and watchtowers.

BERGERAC
[See Major Towns, page 39]

BERNARDIÈRES, CHÂTEAU DES
[DORDOGNE]

This château, 10km NE of Mareuil on the D708 road to Nontron, is open in July, August and September and is well worth seeing. It is built above the river Nizonne around a square, fourteenth-century keep. Vast walls and a dry moat kept out even the redoubtable Du Guesclin when he besieged it in 1377. The château is made up of a central living pavilion above stepped terraces and around a square tower linked by ruined walls and ramparts with a Henri II-style gateway. The main buildings are from the seventeenth century. A frequent visitor was 'Brantôme' – Pierre de Bourdeilles, abbot, wit, envoy of Henri II and Chamberlain to Charles IX and Henri III, who appointed himself a sort of court reporter under the pseudonym of 'Brantôme', writing witty and often scurrilous stories of court scandals, intrigues and junketings.

BESSE
[DORDOGNE]

Tiny village in the Quercy Forest, between the Dordogne river and the Lot, E of the D710. A delightful area of secretive hamlets, pretty lanes and little streams, it is reminiscent of the Dordogne and Lot countryside of forty years ago, before tourism was encouraged. It has an interesting fortified Romanesque church roofed with stone slates. The belfry porch has an unusual, carved eleventh-century doorway. Simple figures depict daringly the Seven Deadly Sins, scenes in the Garden of Eden, an angel with the lamb, and hunting scenes.

BEYNAC-ET-CAZENAC
[DORDOGNE]

Beynac is still my favourite village on the Dordogne, though many people have joined me there since I used to stay in the 1950s to walk, eat, drink, sleep and to fish in one of the most beautiful stretches of the Dordogne river.

I stayed at one of those old-style Périgord inns, the Bonnet, run for generations by the family of the same name, and as I sat on their terrace looking at the river just across the road hardly a vehicle passed. Just occasionally, I could hear a car climbing the steep narrow hill to the great medieval castle standing on a rock 150 metres above us, commanding the whole bank of the river for miles. I was fit enough, then, to walk up between the houses and along the cliff path.

The Bonnet is still there, run by the little girl who was the granddaughter in the 1950s – Mademoiselle Renée Bonnet – and the food is as good, the portions as big. The only difference is that there are now many cars climbing the hill to the castle, which is near to being completely restored, and a new shop has appeared selling Dordogne wine and local specialities to tourists.

From the old ferry pier, pleasure boats take tourists up and down the river in summer. But once the day-tourists have gone, Beynac can be as cosy and almost as quiet as when I found it, and the Dordogne is as beautiful. I suppose nostalgia plays a part in my love for it.

The castle is magnificent and frightening. It has been called brutal, but was built up there, of course, to control the valley and the river, and it has the most magnificent views. You can see for miles along the river, as it winds and snakes between the hills, which are topped with castles – Marqueyssac, La Malartrie, pretty Fayrac and the once-mighty Castelnaud, the hated enemy of Beynac, which is now being restored.

The castle was built in the twelfth century for a crusader Lord of Beynac. When he died Richard Coeur de Lion took it and put in a thug called Mercadier who pillaged the countryside and became heartily hated throughout Périgord.

In 1214, the equally hated Simon de Montfort, on his 'crusade' to wipe out the men, women and children of the Albigensian religious sect, accused the castle's owner of being sympathetic to the sect, seized the castle and dismantled most of it. But the Lord of Beynac rebuilt it before the century was out.

Beynac was one of the four powerful baronies of Périgord, with Biron (see page 87), Bourdeilles (page 88) and Mareuil (page 134). The importance of the castle commanding the river was heightened by the fact that it is only 10km SW of Sarlat. In the Hundred Years War (1337–1453) it was part of the lands ceded to the English by the Treaty of Brétigny in 1360, but eight years later it was retaken by the French King's forces and became the French front line, with the English holding Castelnaud over the river until 1453. The men holding the castles could see the other one, and they sent out raiding parties regularly, which looted and pillaged nearby villages. Living in the village below the castle was far from peaceful in those days.

The castle has been restored very carefully by the State Beaux Arts department. Crumbling stone has been replaced by that from quarries used in the fourteenth century. The cobbled stone floors have also been beautifully replaced.

There is a sheer drop of 150 metres on three sides of the castle, which was also protected by a double perimeter wall, a double moat and a powerful quadrangular tower. Among the rooms are a beautiful barrel-vaulted great hall, called Salle d'État because the nobles of Périgord held their council meetings in it. A seventeenth-century stone Florentine staircase has been restored and a magnificent spiral wooden staircase has been reconstructed from fifty-year-old oak slabs, with each step – tread and riser – sculpted in one piece. A fifteenth-century chapel has a fresco of the Beynac family and another of the Last Supper. The kitchen, still being restored, has a convenient chute for pouring '*confiture*' (boiling oil) on Englishmen trying to drop in for dinner.

There are splendid panoramic views from the castle sentry-path and from a Calvary on the cliff edge 150 metres from the castle.

In Cazenac hamlet, just NW, is a fifteenth-century church. 2km SE at Vézac is Château de Marqueyssac.

HOTELS

Bonnet (53.29.50.01). See text. ROOMS D. MEALS C–F. Open 15 April–15 October.

Taverne des Remparts, place du Château (53.29.57.76). Only four rooms. Opposite château. True Perigordian dishes. ROOMS C. MEALS A–F. Shut 1 November–1 March.

BEYSSAC, CHÂTEAU DE
[DORDOGNE]

On the beautiful D47 E of Les Eyzies towards Sarlat you can see on your left above the oak forest the impressive sixteenth-century Château de Beyssac, with a machicolated tower. Around the château are some abandoned seventeenth- to eighteenth-century forges. 1km E a path to the right takes you to Breuil, a Gaulish village with a group of tiny stone huts unchanged since the Neolithic Stone Age.

BIRON, CHÂTEAU
[DORDOGNE]

Château Biron is one of the bulkiest and most dominating châteaux in France. Eight km SW of Monpazier, it perches on top of a stone knoll. Biron has had a turbulent history and owes its survival to its mass of strong walls and towers, and to the Gontaut family who owned it and added to it on and off through fourteen generations until the French Government took it over this century and opened it to the public.

It was attacked, captured, recaptured, partly knocked down, repaired, enlarged and strengthened through almost each generation, so that it became a group of fortresses, so untidy that some seem to be built almost on top of others. It is very commanding and its village is delightful.

The château was started in the twelfth century. Early in the thirteenth century it was in the hands of the Albigensian sect, or at least the infamous Simon de Montfort claimed that it was, and he took it in 1233. King Louis VIII gave it back to Gontauts, who played the English and the French against each other. The Plantagenets held it for the English from 1239 to 1294. It was of great importance in the Hundred Years War and after the Earl of Derby took it in 1345 it changed hands between French and English several times. After 1463 the Gontauts were able to rebuild in peace. Biron was one of the four great baronies of Périgord. Henri IV raised it to a Duchy in 1598 as a reward for the fine soldier Armand de Gontaut-Biron who fought for Henri III against Henri IV when he was Henri de Navarre, the Protestant leader. Armand negotiated peace terms between them, then fought for Henri IV against the extremist Catholic League. He had his head blown off at the Siege of Epernay. His son Charles was made Marshal of France and Governor of Burgundy by Henri IV, but that was not enough for him and he plotted with the King of Spain to break up France. Henri forgave him, but he did it again and was beheaded for treason at Les Tuileries. The family got back their title of Lords of Biron in 1723.

Biron is well worth visiting for its cavalcade of different styles of architecture. The Renaissance buildings, the pavilion, the stables and eighteenth-century cloisters add charm to the old fighting fortress. The village is within the outer walls. Inside the main gateway is a large grassy courtyard, big enough to take all the villagers and their livestock in times of trouble. From here you can enter the bottom part of the masterpiece of the château, the chapel. This bottom chapel was used by the servants and the villagers and is still the village church. The upper chapel was for the family and their guests. The tombs of Pons Gontaut, who had the chapel built, and his brother Armand, Bishop of Sarlat, who built Sarlat church, are superbly designed and made. To the indignation of local people, the last Duke sold two of the chapel's main treasures to New York's Metropolitan Museum, although they were classified historic monuments. The state hall, the fine monumental staircase and the huge, stone-slabbed kitchen are delightful.

BORIES, CHÂTEAU DES
[*See* Antonne-et-Trigonant, page 71]

BOURDEILLES, CHÂTEAU DE
[DORDOGNE]

This château, one of the four great baronies of Périgord, is a superb example of a medieval château built for war, and then converted into a Renaissance palace for living in. Although the Bourdeilles family no longer reside in it, they did offer it to the State, which has restored it, filled it with furniture (albeit partly Spanish) and opened it to the public and for musical concerts.

10km downstream from Brantôme, on a rocky spur above the Dronne river, Bourdeilles has a very tall eight-sided keep from the thirteenth-century medieval castle. Built by Gérard de Maumont, this older part is called the 'new château' because it was built on the foundations of a still-older castle. It all came about because King Louis IX (St Louis) ceded the baronies of Périgord and of Bourdeilles to the English, which made the

Bourdeilles

Bourdeilles locals furious and split the Bourdeilles family. The elders supported the English Plantagenets. The younger branch, the Maumonts, supported the French kings. The Maumonts seized the twelfth-century castle and built the new fortress. The new French king, Philippe IV (Philip the Fair), turned Bourdeilles into a strong fortress inside English-owned territory. It is a mass of fortifications grouped round the keep, inside great ramparts topped by a machicolated sentry-walk.

The keep has walls some three metres thick, with a vaulted room on each floor and a spiral staircase to the upper platform. From here is a lovely view of the castle below, the village under the walls, and a curved medieval bridge beside an old fortified watermill built like a ship. Its wheels still turn.

The Renaissance house was built in a hurry by Jacquette de Montbron, wife of Comte André de Bourdeilles and sister-in-law of Pierre de Bourdeilles, the soldier-satirist who used the name Brantôme and wrote such amusing scandal about court ladies (*see* Brantôme, *below*). Jacquette was expecting a visit from Catherine de' Medici, who was taking her young son Charles to see something of his kingdom. Jacquette built the new house for Catherine's court, but Catherine did not arrive, so Jacquette stopped building. However, she had already built a lovely house, as well as the Golden Chamber, sumptuously decorated by André Le Nôtre of the Fontainebleau school of court artists, including a magnificent French ceiling. Most of the furniture came from Château de la Trayne. There are corsairs' sea chests and a superb tapestry of Francois I with his falconers. The Spanish furnishings and paintings on the second floor include the sculpted and gilded bed of the Emperor Charles V.

HOTEL

Griffons (53.03.75.61). Sixteenth-century house by the medieval bridge. Comfortable, quiet. Beautiful interior. ROOMS F. MEALS D–G. Open early April–30 September.

BRANTÔME
[DORDOGNE]

One of the most delightful towns in France, even in midsummer when the crowds roll in and there are parking problems. Try to visit in May, early June or September when it is a joy.

Enfolded by two arms of the Dronne river, it is a wonderful place to wander through narrow streets and old squares rich in medieval and Renaissance buildings. It is delightful to dawdle under the shade of willows, lean on stone bridges and watch the river flowing lazily and tumbling over the narrow pier, to stop and admire riverside gardens. You will find many treasures here – the old abbot's garden with rose beds and a pretty Renaissance pavilion, for instance (reached by a sixteenth-century dog-leg bridge), in which 'Brantôme' wrote his amusing satire; also the romantic riverside mill, Moulin de l'Abbaye, which Régis Bulot turned into such a charming hotel.

Charlemagne built the Benedictine abbey here in AD769, but the Norsemen sailed up the Dordogne, as they did almost every sizeable river in France, and ransacked the abbey, as they did all the rest. It was rebuilt in the eleventh century, then altered in the fourteenth and eighteenth centuries. The monastic buildings are now used as the town hall, museum and school, so they are open to the public only from 1 June to 15 September. The seventeenth-century staircase is lovely, but the museum lacks interest except, perhaps, for the amateurish pictures by a local nineteenth-century artist, Fernand Desmoulin, who claimed to have painted under the influence of a medium. He picked the wrong medium.

The church is open and so is its graceful, eleventh-century belltower, which is square, gabled and built on a rock 12 metres above the river. It has four storeys with round arches and is roofed in stone slates.

Caves in the rocks behind the abbey were used by the monks as kitchens and a wine cellar, and the monks carved huge religious scenes in bas-relief on the walls, including one of the Last Judgement – a warning perhaps against gluttony and drunkenness.

Among the joys of Brantôme are the shops selling Perigordian delicacies, such as duck and goose pâtés and *confits*, the old-style cafés and restaurants, and the wonderful Friday food market in the squares. In spring and autumn the market is for the local people and for the farmers who bring in their own lovely farm-fresh produce. In autumn it is splendid for *chanterelles*, *cèpes* and *morilles* mushrooms.

The abbey is remembered for 'Brantôme' (Pierre de Bourdeilles), the sixteenth-century wit who chronicled scandals and gossip of both the court and the battlefields. The son of a Count who had considerable influence at court, he was made a 'commendatory' abbot at sixteen by Henri II – a sinecure to give him an income. He never took Holy Orders. In fact he became a soldier of fortune, and a courtier. He was chosen in 1561 to escort young Mary Stuart back to Scotland after her husband, the young King François II of France, died. Then he went to Malta to fight with the Knights of St John when the island was invaded by Suleiman the Magnificent and afterwards fought in

Brantôme

Italy for the French, in Africa for the Spaniards against the Moors, and in Hungary against the invading Turks. He became Chamberlain to Charles IX and Henri II and fought against the Protestants at Jarnac. But he was crippled by a fall from his horse and returned to Brantôme Abbey to take up at last his duties as abbot and write his chronicles. Because of his contacts and diplomatic persuasion, he twice saved the abbey from being destroyed by the Protestants in the Wars of Religion. He died in Brantôme in 1614.

He is buried nearby (7km NW) in Château de Richemont (*see* page 154), which is worth visiting. Brantôme is a superb centre for touring. Château de Bourdeilles (*see* page 88) is only 10km away down a very attractive route by the D78, then the D106 SW. The route runs alongside the river Dronne where it is lined with poplars and walnut trees and passes under cliffs with shelters used by prehistoric men. 6km NE, Champagnac-de-Belair (*see* page 104) has the magnificent little Moulin du Roc hotel-restaurant. Beautiful Château de Puyguilhem (*see* Villars, page 191) is 9km NE.

TOURIST INFORMATION Pavilion Renaissance (1 April–mid-October – 53.05.80.52)

MARKET Friday

HOTELS

Moulin de l'Abbaye (53.05.80.22). Romantic, ravishing, beautifully furnished fifteenth-century mill. Régis Bulot, fine chef and owner, is sometimes busy elsewhere but young chef Christian Ravel, who was at Troisgros and also with the Roux Brothers at the Waterside, Bray, is one of the best young chefs in France. Expensive but worth it. ROOMS G. MEALS F–G. Open early May–31 October. Restaurant shut Monday.

Chabrol (53.05.70.15). Delightful position by river-bridge. Local institution run by the noted Charbonnel brothers. Splendid meals, enormous choice, lovely wine list. ROOMS E–F. MEALS D–G. Shut 16–28 February; 15 November–10 December; Sunday evening, Monday low season.

Soir, rue Georges-Saumande (53.05.82.93). A personal favourite which has become popular in season. ROOMS B–D. MEALS B–F. Shut 10 January–20 February; Monday in winter.

RESTAURANT

Jurande, 28 rue Victor Hugo (53.05.78.22). Small, friendly. Regional dishes. MEALS A–G. Shut Tuesday evening, Wednesday.

BRIDOIRE, CHÂTEAU DE
[DORDOGNE]

Just S of Monbazillac and 12km S of Bergerac, the château de Bridoire is a fine fifteenth- to sixteenth-century building in grey stone, not unlike Château de Monbazillac itself (*see* page 138). It still has great round battlemented towers, but once had a massive outer wall. An earlier castle belonged to Marguerite de Turenne in 1274. Last century Charles de Foucauld lived at

Bridoire after restoring it. A French cavalry officer living a dissipated life, he saw the light and became a helper of the poor and then a hermit in Algeria, where he was murdered in 1916. His mission (Mission de Charles) is still at work.

BRIVE
[*See* Major Towns, page 43]

LE BUGUE
[DORDOGNE]

A happy, lively market town on the river Vézère near where it joins the Dordogne, which is described by a French friend as '*coquette*'. Only 11km W of Les Eyzies. The road from Périgueux crosses the Vézère and continues southward over the Dordogne to the charming area of the Bessède Forest known to very few visitors. I love it.

Bugue has a super market every Tuesday and Saturday morning and a series of lively old-style Dordogne fairs. There are some delightful Renaissance houses with iron balconies which give them a slightly Spanish look.

It has good watersports facilities, campsites and international show-jumping in August at Parc Royal Vézère.

Just 1km W along D703 is the prehistoric cave of Bara-Bahau, discovered only in 1951 by the prehistorian Norbert Casteret. Created by an underground river, the cave is 120 metres long with engravings of horses, oxen, bison and rhinoceroses made about 20,000–30,000 years ago. They are difficult to decipher.

Gouffre de Proumeyssac chasm is 3½km S. It has fine stalagmites and stalactites and a stream running through it – all beautifully lit. Both caves are open from Palm Sunday–30 September.

TOURIST INFORMATION Le Bugue Hôtel-de-Ville
(53.07.20.48 – in season)
MARKETS Tuesday, Saturday morning

Le Bugue

FAIRS Third Tuesday of every month
MAIN FAIRS 25 August, 30 September
FESTIVAL First Sunday in July – Félibrée, traditional
festival

HOTELS

Royal Vézère l'Albuca, place Hôtel-de-Ville (hotel 53.07.20.01; restaurant *Albuca* 53.07.28.73). Beside the river with roof terrace, swimming-pool, disco. Regional dishes and fish. Also cheaper restaurant *Le Jardin Albuca*. ROOMS E–G. MEALS C–G. *Le Jardin* MEALS A–C. Open early April–early October. Restaurant shut Monday, Tuesday lunch.

Auberge Noyer, Le Réclaud de Bouny Bas, 5km W on D703 (53.07.11.73). Lovely eighteenth-century farmhouse made into an inn by English couple – Jenny and Paul Dyer. Quiet wooded garden, swimming-pool. ROOMS D–E. MEALS A–E. Shut 31 October–31 March except New Year. Restaurant shut Monday and Tuesday lunch.

See also Campagne (page 98).

LE BUISSON
[DORDOGNE]

Pleasant town on D31 just after it crosses the Dordogne river S of Le Bugue. Important as a rail junction and shopping centre for local villages, it has a good campsite, river beaches for bathing and sunbathing, and some good, cheap restaurants.

MARKET Friday

BUSSIÈRE-BADIL
[DORDOGNE]

Very beautiful eleventh-century church with superb porch in this medieval town in the NW corner of Dordogne, 18km NW of Nontron, near the Charente border. Inside is a sixteenth-century coloured statue of the Virgin and Child carved by Mathieu Dyonise of Le Mans.

The village green runs down to the small river Tardoire with an old wash-house.

CADOUIN
[DORDOGNE]

A village on the edge of the charming and quiet Bessède Forest, S from Le Buisson and Le Bugue. A Cistercian abbey, founded in 1115, is still there, beautifully restored by the State. Two years after it was founded, the Bishop of Puy gave the monks a piece of ancient cloth which was said to have covered the face of Christ

Cadouin Abbey

in the tomb. It had been found hidden in the wall of a church in Antioch. For centuries the abbey was a famous place of pilgrimage. St Louis (Louis IX of France), Richard Coeur de Lion of England and the Emperor Charles V all came to kneel before it. In the Hundred Years War, when the English threatened the abbey, the monks sent the holy shroud for safety to Toulouse and then Aubazines. It took them many lawsuits and the help of the Pope and Louis XI to get it back. It was Louis who gave them the money to start rebuilding their cloisters destroyed in the war. In 1934 experts decided that the holy shroud was not genuine. The embroidered bands bore Arab inscriptions of the eleventh century.

The cloisters were not finished until the sixteenth century, a hundred years after they were started, so Flamboyant Gothic cloisters have some lovely Renaissance touches and sculpted decorations on the abbot's stone seat. The wall alongside has a striking fresco of the Annunciation. There are doors at each corner. One is adorned with the arms of France and Brittany in recognition of Anne of Brittany, a benefactress of the abbey who married two kings of France, Charles VIII and Louis XII. These

lovely cloisters and their garden were not badly damaged in the
Revolution; and were well restored after the State took over in
1839.

The church itself is huge, but austere and dark inside. A
museum of religious art is next to the abbey. In the village is an
old people's home in lovely Périgord style.

Cadouin is right on the edge of Bessède Forest and the lanes
around it take you to hamlets and farms where the old farming
life continues almost unaffected by tourism. The little D28 to
Badefols-sur-Dordogne is very attractive and joins the equally
attractive D29 along the south bank of the river to the bridge to
Lalinde, from which there are good river views.

CALVIAC
[See Carlux, page 99]

CAMPAGNE
[DORDOGNE]

Just SE of Le Bugue at a meeting of pretty roads near the
Vézère river, Campagne has a highly restored fifteenth-century
château made of two buildings facing each other, joined at the
ends by a square keep and a square wing. Two round towers
flank the north side. It is in a fine park. Much of the château is
used as a store by Les Eyzies museum.

The village is pretty and has a twelfth-century church, communal washing basin with a fine balustrade, and a very pleasant
hostellerie.

HOTEL
Château (53.07.23.50). Friendly, comfortable hotel. Well-
furnished rooms with terrace. Many menus. ROOMS C–D.
MEALS A–G. Open early April–31 October.

CARLUX
[Dordogne]

Just N of the Dordogne river between Sarlat and Souillac, Carlux is the centre of some delightful little roads running N to real farming villages unknown to tourists and attractive roads on both banks of the river. There are fine walks around here, too. Its own château, burned by the English in the Hundred Years War, is still a ruin, but there are some fine châteaux nearby, including Fénelon (*see* page 118), Montfort (page 143) and Rouffilhac 2½km S by the river-bridge. The much-restored château of Rouffilhac is on a lovely hillside of evergreen oaks above the Dordogne river. 3km along the right riverbank by the attractive D703 is Calviac-en-Périgord, which has pretty houses grouped round the church, originally part of a twelfth-century abbey, but considerably embellished later. Here lived the monk Sacerdos, beatified for curing leprosy, and made patron saint of Sarlat.

Another 3km along the river is Carsac-Aillac, a ravishing stone-tiled village with its partly stone-roofed Château de la Gazaille among a grove of lime trees with a remarkable little church built in golden stone. Its massive Romanesque belfry and its apse are roofed in stone. Inside, beside the primitive Romanesque capitals, is Gothic vaulting. At the east end are some very modern stained glass and a Stations of the Cross, with texts from the writings of the diplomat-author Paul Claudel, who died in 1955. From the corniche outside the village is a lovely view over the great loop in the river, Cingle de Montfort.

There are several campsites in this area. Ombrages de Dordogne at Rouffilhac (65.29.70.24) is small but pleasant.

HOTEL
Poissons Frais (53.29.70.24). Nice view. ROOMS C. MEALS A–F. Shut October.

CASTELNAUD, CHÂTEAU DE
[DORDOGNE]

The hated enemy of Beynac – the castle which the English held for most of the Hundred Years War – is being restored. Soon it will be ready for visitors.

Castelnaud stands on a spur completely dominating the rivers Céon and Dordogne as far as Beynac, which you can see from the terrace beyond a great river loop. Below it, down the hillside are the old village houses. The Cazenac family built it in the twelfth century. But it 1214 Simon de Montfort decided that he liked it, so he accused the family of supporting the Albigensian sect and took it from them. He did not, however, knock it down, as he did most other castles after looting them. The family took it back the following year.

When the English took it in the Hundred Years War, it was

Château de Castelnaud

commanded for twenty-five years by the great soldier Raymond de Sort. The English made it much stronger, with a keep and barbican.

In the Wars of Religion, a melodrama was played out which few writers of historical novels would have dared to invent. The younger son of Castelnaud's Lord, Geoffroy de Caumont, who was Abbot of Clairac in Agenais, had secretly become a Protestant. When both his father and elder brother died, he inherited Castelnaud. So he left the Catholic Church officially and married a widow, Marguerite de Lustrac, who was known as Madame la Maréchale because her first husband had been Maréchal de St André. In 1572 Geoffroy died mysteriously of 'mushroom poisoning'. Three months later his widow gave birth to a daughter Anne, who was a very rich heiress.

Her uncle, Jean de Cars, was appointed her guardian by King Henri III. With his eye on the money, he determined to marry her to his son Prince de Carency. But the more-powerful Lord of Biron was after her for *his* son. So Jean de Cars kidnapped the seven-year-old girl and forcibly married her to the Prince. Five years later her eighteen-year-old husband was killed by none other than eighteen-year-old Charles de Biron. Anne was a rich twelve-year-old widow. Jean de Cars tried to marry her to his second son. Madame la Maréchale put a stop to it by enlisting the help of the Protestant captain Geoffroy de Vivans, who was born nearby, and of the Duc de Mayenne, military commander of the Catholic League. The Duke also wanted Anne's fortune, so he kidnapped her and made her marry his son in Paris. The boy was only nine years old.

Henri III stepped in and sent her to be looked after by the religious Catholic Duchess of Nemours, who converted Anne to Catholicism.

At eighteen she was again kidnapped and married for a third time to François d'Orléans, Count of St Pol. They had a son, but St Pol was a lecher and wastrel and she left him, taking her son who became a page to Louis XIII. He was killed at the Siege of Montpellier. Anne retired to a convent, to the fury of Madame la Maréchale who disinherited her and gave Castelnaud to Anne's cousin Jacques de Caumont to keep it in the family.

After the Revolution, roofs fell in and the stones were stolen to make other buildings.

See also Châteaux de Fayrac (page 117) and des Milandes (page 137).

CAUDON
[*See* Cénac, *below*]

CÉNAC-ET-ST-JULIEN
[DORDOGNE]

Cénac straggles along the road beneath the cliff on which the medieval town of Domme stands. It is known these days for bathing in the Dordogne, its market, campsites and its August wine festival held in the streets. Once it had the important Priory of St Julien, finished in the twelfth century. The small Romanesque church is all that remains. Much was destroyed by the Protestants serving under Geoffroy de Vivans (born nearby at Château de Fayrac) after he had taken the 'impregnable' Domme. The whole was heavily restored last century. The carvings inside are interesting and fun. The tops of the capitals have carvings of lions, rabbits, monkeys and birds, said to be some of the finest animal carvings of the Romanesque period. The human beings include Daniel (and the Lion), a man scratching the back and neck of monkeys, two women watching Lazarus raised from the tomb and holding their noses against the smell, and men and women dancing naked and clothed. A snake between two women warns against lust. Carvings in the churchyard are very medieval – a lion eats his prey, a pig eats human heads, a man shows his backside, a man and woman are in a lewd clinch.

In the fourteenth century, the Prior of St Julien refused entrance to the Bishop of Bordeaux after an argument. Alas for him, the Bishop became Pope Clément V and excommunicated him from the Catholic Church!

Cénac

The pretty hamlet of St Julien was the port of Cénac and Domme in the days of Dordogne *gabare* traffic. Château de Fondaumier to the west was the home of Albéric Cahuet, the nineteenth-century novelist who set several stories in the area, including *Pontcarral*, the story of a Napoleonic colonel and his problems returning to civil life after adventures with the Emperor at Austerlitz and Moscow.

At Caudon, 4km NE on D50, is a troglodyte medieval church in a cave with a belltower and bells.

MARKET Cénac: Tuesday

FESTIVAL Two days in August – Cénac Wine Festival

HOTEL

Guerinière, Cénac (53.28.22.44). Calm and relaxation in an eighteenth-century former abbey. Gardens and terrace with views of Domme high above. ROOMS E–F. MEALS D–G. Shut 15 November–15 March; Tuesday low season.

RESTAURANT

La Ferme, Caudon-de-Vitrac (53.28.33.35). Goodness knows how many years ago it was that I lunched here when Maurice Escalier had just opened his big farmhouse kitchen and dining room as a restaurant and almost everything came from the farm. I ate far too much, drank even more and paid very little. He still starts with soup, bread and garlic. He offers much more choice now, but still true farmhouse dishes in generous portions. MEALS A–F. Shut October; 19–26 December; Monday.

CHAMPAGNAC-DE-BELAIR
[DORDOGNE]

In a lovely area on D83 NE of Brantôme, the village is on a spur overlooking the Dronne river and its valley. The seventeenth-century Château de la Borie-Saulnier replaced one destroyed in 1569 by Protestants. It has a fine sixteenth-century church.

An important market is held on the first Monday of each month, and some of the best meals in Dordogne are served at the delightful Moulin du Roc, converted from an old walnut-oil mill. The garden beside the little river is a delight, the bedrooms sumptuously furnished, the service perfect.

MARKET First Monday of each month
FESTIVAL Last Sunday in August – Sheep Fair

HOTEL

Moulin du Roc (53.54.80.36). See text. One of my favourites in France. Solange Gardillou is possibly France's best female chef. Book well ahead. ROOMS F–G. MEALS F–G. Shut 15 November–15 December; 15 January–15 February. Restaurant shut Wednesday lunch, Tuesday.

CHAMPAGNE-ET-FONTAINE
[DORDOGNE]

SW of Mareuil on D24. Sixteenth-century Renaissance Château de Clauzurou with living quarters flanked by two taller wings, the three enclosing a courtyard reached through an eighteenth-century gateway. The tops of its towers were knocked off in the Revolution. A twelfth-century church was fortified in the Wars of Religion.

CHAMPEAUX
and
LA CHAPELLE-POMMIER
[DORDOGNE]

The country NW of the D939 Mareuil-Brantôme road (the old Nontronnais–Riberacois road) is little explored by visitors but has some very pleasant old villages and châteaux, and attractive scenery. These villages are on a local road joining Vieux-Mareuil on the D939 to the D708 are typical. Champeaux has a nice twelfth-century church, so has La Chapelle-Pommier. Château des Bernardières (*see* page 83), built in the twelfth century and altered in the eighteenth, was one which the writer Brantôme used to visit.

CHANCELADE ABBEY
[DORDOGNE]

A few km NW of Périgueux on the D710, the village of Chancelade grew around a twelfth-century abbey where the Beauronne river flows through hills. The abbey buildings still remaining are a delightful deconsecrated Romanesque chapel, the abbot's dwellings, and the handsome abbey church with a really lovely belltower. Frescos in the chancel show St Christopher and St Thomas à Becket, the Archbishop of Canterbury who was murdered on the steps of his cathedral.

A museum of sacred art (open afternoons 1 June to 30 September) is housed in a room of the old abbey house, now the presbytery, and around a courtyard are a laundry room, stables, workshop and a fortified mill. Adjoining this is the garden, overlooked by the abbey house with two turrets (open afternoons 1 June to 30 September). Though the abbey was badly damaged in wars, the monks continued repairing and building until the Revolution.

LE CHANGÉ
[DORDOGNE]

A lovely village on a bend in the river Auvézère, 17km E of Périgueux. Its houses nestle round the fifteenth-century manor house (Château de la Sandre), which has a thirteenth-century tower, the fifteenth-century Château de la Faurie, with a round battlemented tower, and a Romanesque church in good repair. Across the old bridge is a charming ancient mill.

LA CHAPELLE-FAUCHER
[DORDOGNE]

E of Brantôme on the D3, S of Champagnac-de-Belair, romantic ruins of this fifteenth-century château, which burnt down when struck by lightning, can be seen on a cliff above the river Côle. Two massive towers with sentry-walks are still inhabited. Modest, twelfth-century domed church.

CHAUMEIL
[CORRÈZE]

The Massif de Monédières is in a sort of no man's land SW of
Treignac between the D940 and D16, and Chaumeil is in the SE
corner. It is the capital of Monédières and has a population of
275! If you seek country to explore away from crowds, this is
surely your place. Take the D940, a lovely road which runs into
Corrèze through Bourganeuf, Peyrat and Eymoutiers, to Treignac, turn left on the equally lovely D16 for 10km just past
Lestards. Turn right on the little D32 to Chaumeil. There is a
lagoon (*étang*) just before you reach it. Its strong granite houses
are around the village church, in which there are a naïve poly-
chrome Pietà (sixteenth century) displayed under lighting, and a
Madonna and Child.

For an attractive route round the massif take the narrow
D121 W to the tiny hamlet of Freysselines where it winds along a
south slope among chestnut groves to Chauzeix. Take the road
climbing right, then right again on to the rising D128. On the
left is the long ridge of Puy Pantout (770 metres) then on the
right the wooded slope of Puy de Chauzeix (893 metres). Left is
Puy de la Monédière, the tallest peak in the massif at 919 metres
and just an eroded mass of crystalline rock.

At Col du Bos pass take the D128E right to Suc-au-May
where a ten-minute walk takes you to the viewing table at 908
metres. From here is a panorama of the Corrèze countryside,
the Millevaches Plateau NE, Monts Doré and Dômes E. Return
to D128 and at Col des Géants Pass you can turn right on D32 to
Chaumeil or left to Treignac.

Massif des Monédières was twice a forest. When Caesar
invaded, druids hid in it to organize a resistance. Caesar ordered
the forest to be burned, and the fire lasted several months.
Medieval monks patiently replanted. In the sixteenth century
the local lord, Louis de Pompadour, the powerful Baron of
Treignac, was a Catholic, his neighbours mostly Protestant.
When they entered his domaine, he set light to the forest again
over an area of thirty square miles, burning villages, crops and
castles. The Protestants left but Louis had ruined himself.

Reafforestation has been very difficult. Recently it has increased and some hillsides are covered, but with conifers.

East of Chaumeil is Le Mas Michel, a hamlet of dry-stone cottages well worth visiting.

HOTEL

Bruyères, Chaumeil (55.21.34.68). Logis de France with fourteen rooms and good cooking by Madame Feugeas. ROOMS C. MEALS A–C. Shut 5–31 January; 10–25 October.

CLERMONT-DE-BEAUREGARD
[DORDOGNE]

On the D21 NE of Bergerac, where vines begin to give way to strawberries, is the beautiful fifteenth-century Château de Gaubertie, restored early in the twentieth century. A single-storey building, it has one façade (overlooking the valley) flanked by square and round corbelled towers, the other façade by a big round tower. A sentry-walk runs round the top. Dormer windows break the tiled roof. Do not muddle it with the equally beautiful Château de la Jaubertie at Colombier where superb wine is made (*see* Monbazillac, page 138).

COLLONGES-LA-ROUGE
[CORRÈZE]

Called 'la Rouge' for the dark-red stone of its mansions, old cottages and twelfth-century fortified church, this charming old town is reached along the D38 from Brive through wooded hills and valleys planted with walnuts and vines. Any place so beautiful is certain to draw many visitors in high summer, so leave your car at the former railway station on the main road and walk. (Cars are forbidden to go any further from June to mid-September.)

You reach a sixteenth-century corbelled house with a lovely

stone roof decorated with the figure of a little Siren playing a lute. It was called Maison de la Sirène, but no one knows now who she was. This one looks like a mermaid.

The big mansion topped with two turrets was the town house of the powerful Ramade de Friac family. Past the Relais de St Jacques-de-Compostelle, through a covered passage in the old walls and an alley, is a winding road down to a fortified mansion, Hôtel de Beuges. The road opposite the Relais leads to the eleventh- to twelfth-century church, which was fortified in the Wars of Religion by strengthening the great square keep with a gun-room that connected with the watch-sentry on the battlements. Along rue de Garde, past the church, is the elegant but highly fortified Castel de Vassignac, built in 1583 for Gédéon de Vassignac, who then ruled Collonges as captain-governor for the Viscount of Turenne. This viscountcy remained virtually self-ruling from the sixteenth century until one of the viscounts sold his rights to Louis XV, to the annoyance of the peasants, who had until then avoided having to pay tithes to the church which left them poverty-stricken (*see* Turenne, page 181).

The 'castel' bristles with towers and turrets, defensive loop-holes for firing, and watch-towers. A more domestic touch is the communal oven in the covered market. Try to stay overnight and see the town romantically lit by illuminations in season or by moonlight at other times.

HOTELS

Relais St Jacques-de-Compostelle (55.25.41.02). Superb old inn with charming terrace. ROOMS B–D. MEALS C–G. Shut 1 December–31 January; Tuesday evening, Wednesday in winter.
Auberge Le Prieuré (55.25.41.00). Charming flower-decked house; excellent value. Simple rooms. Real regional dishes. ROOMS B–C. MEALS A–D. Shut 1 December–15 March.

COLOMBIER
[*See* Monbazillac, page 139]

CORGNAC-SUR-L'ISLE
[DORDOGNE]

A small village, SE of Thiviers, near the N21, with a fine medieval bridge over the Isle river and magnificent fortress, Château de Laxion, built strictly for warfare during the Wars of Religion by one of the Rastignac family. It is said to have been unaltered since it was built and certainly looks dilapidated, although still formidable.

CORRÈZE
[CORRÈZE]

Ancient town 5km N of the N89 Tulle–Ussel road, near the Corrèze gorge. Ramparts, an ancient gate (Porte Margot) and houses from the fifteenth and sixteenth centuries remain. Nearby is the lagoon Étang de Meyrignac-l'Église.

HOTEL
Séniorie, place Mairie (55.21.22.88). Attractive, quiet hotel in old house. ROOMS E–G. MEALS D–F. Shut 2 January–2 February. Restaurant shut Sunday evening, Monday.

COULAURES
[DORDOGNE]

Beautiful little town which was once important because it overlooked the meeting of the Isle and Loue rivers, 6km SW of Excideuil. Its many old buildings include a well-restored Romanesque church with two domes and fourteenth-century fresco inside, a seventeenth-century chapel of Notre-Dame-du-Pont and two châteaux – Château de la Cousse (sixteenth to seventeenth century) and Château de Couty, a riverside mansion built in 1830 around a much older square, battlemented tower.

COURSAC
[Dordogne]

8km SW of Périgueux on D4, Coursac has a rather threatening battlemented château – la Jarthe. It was the home of the Du Puy family who supplied Périgueux with more than thirty mayors.

COUZE-ET-ST-FRONT
[Dordogne]

The D660 E from Bergerac along the Dordogne crosses the river from Port-de-Couze to Couze-et-St-Front, which may have been the birthplace of St Front, the missionary who converted much of Périgord to Christianity. Dordogne's most important paper-making centre, they have made paper here since the fifteenth century and there are schools for hand paper-making. It specializes these days in filter papers. The twelfth-century Chapel of St Front lies to the E (*see* Lalinde, page 129), and W along the D37 is Château de Lanquais (*see* page 131).
MARKET Monday

CUREMONTE
[Corrèze]

A typical old fortified hilltop village of Corrèze, its fine châteaux and mansions with flat-tiled roofs surrounded by ramparts can be seen for miles across the Causse de Martel. It stands near the little river Sourdoire 10km NW of Beaulieu-sur-Dordogne by tiny roads. Curemonte was built up in the eleventh century under the lords of Turenne.

Opposite the market in the village centre is a calvary with twelve sixteenth-century bas-reliefs showing the life of Jesus. Behind the church the perimeter wall skirts the sixteenth-century Château de la Plas and its round towers, and the fifteenth-century Château de St Hilaire with a square, battle-mented tower. Opposite are sixteenth- to seventeenth-century mansions. There are more old houses in place du Château. You can walk along the ramparts for lovely views over the Martel plateau.

Fewer than 250 people live in Curemonte, but it is a charming little hide-out and I am surprised that more explorers have not found it.

Colette, the writer, fled there to her daughter Bel-Gazou's mansion when the Germans took Paris in 1940, but she was unhappy because she had no petrol, and she called it her 'verd-ant tomb'. A lot of Parisians would have been very glad of such a beautiful bolt-hole.

DOISSAT
[Dordogne]

SE of Belvès on the D34, Doissat has a ruined château where the Protestant captain Geoffroy de Vivans was buried. Part of it is now a walnut museum.

DOMME
[Dordogne]

One of the most beautiful places in France! It stands on a rock crag high above the river Dordogne's left bank, almost opposite La Roque-Gageac. Built in 1280 for the French King Philip the Bold (*le Hardi*), whose boldness was often foolhardiness, it has a panoramic view from its belvedere (*la Barre*), a stone balustrade above a precipitous drop. This is an even better view than those from Beynac and La Roque-Gageac. You can see the Dordogne river lined with willows and poplars winding in a huge loop through fields of corn. Across the river are wooded hills broken occasionally by ochre cliffs. Most days you can see La Roque-Gageac clearly.

An even better view, as far as Beynac castle, can be seen from the new garden at the end of the clifftop path at the west side of town.

The D50 road to Domme winds up from Cénac village (*see* page 102) to Porte del Bos, one of the three remaining gateways. A small street curves under an arch into the bottom square, where you should park. From there, narrow streets climb steeply past beautiful old houses to the top square, place de la Halle, which is surrounded by ochre stone houses. The church is in one corner, the turreted Maison du Gouverneur on the east side, and in the centre is the old market hall with a little balcony on round stone pillars. Below the market is the entrance to caves used as hiding places by the townsfolk in the Hundred Years War and the Wars of Religion. A series of small chambers approximately 450 metres long have been cleared for visits (1 April to 31 October). Some chambers have slender white stalactites and pillars formed from the meeting of stalactites and stalagmites. Bones of bison and rhinoceroses found in the caves are on show.

Domme's beauty lies not only in its location and old buildings but in the colour of the stone in which the buildings are built and the flowers and vines growing up their balconies and outside staircases. The terrace of the Esplanade Hotel where I ate for many years has a river view as good as the food served there.

From Porte del Bos, the town entrance, you can walk inside what is left of the ramparts to reach Porte des Tours, which is flanked by two massive semi-circular towers. In one are names and coats of arms of Knights Templars imprisoned there in the fourteenth century when, under Papal Orders, Philippe le Bel, King of France, arrested nearly all members of the Order in one coup, accused them of appalling crimes to which many confessed under torture, and killed most of them. The Pope banned the ancient Order.

Philip the Bold built Domme to be impregnable. But the Protestant leader Geoffroy de Vivans was born at Château Fayrac, 10km down the Dordogne, and in the Religious Wars he took Domme without disturbing a stone. The vertical cliff face under the Barre was believed to be unclimbable, but with thirty men he climbed it in the night. Inside the sleeping town, his men beat drums, blew trumpets and caused pandemonium. Before the guards could rub their eyes his men opened the gates and let in the Protestant troops. Then, having taken the town, he spoilt his victory by burning the church. In 1592 when his friend Henri of Navarre was King Henri IV of France and all but the hard-line Catholic Leaguers had tired of fighting, Vivans sold Domme back to the Catholics for 40,000 livres.

TOURIST INFORMATION Syndicat d'Initiative, place Halle (shut mornings out of season – 53.28.37.09)
MARKET Thursday morning

HOTEL

Esplanade (53.28.31.41). Superb views over Dordogne, 150 metres below. Pretty bedrooms. Excellent classical cooking. Book ahead. ROOMS D–G. MEALS D–G. Open 14 February–15 November. Restaurant shut Monday.

L'ÉVÊQUE, CHÂTEAU
[DORDOGNE]

On the pretty D939 11km N of Périgueux, the château was a bishop's palace started in the fourteenth century but rebuilt in the sixteenth. The modern neo-Gothic church has some features left of the earlier church where St Vincent de Paul (1581–1660) was ordained. He started charities for the poor, including the foundling hospital in Paris, 'Filles de la Charité'. After his ordination, in 1605, he was captured by pirates on a voyage from Marseilles to Narbonne and was sold in slavery in Tunis to a renegade Savoyard but talked his master into returning to Christianity and escaped back to France.

EXCIDEUIL
[Dordogne]

The lords of Limoges and Périgord, the French and English, the Catholics and Protestants warred over Excideuil and its great fortress-château. Now it is an impressive ruin in a charming town in the attractive, almost forgotten area of Dordogne, NE of Périgueux and W of Hautefort. This is where my wife and I like to hide in *gîtes*. Excideuil is on the attractive D705 near to the Loue river.

What is left of the château is splendid but, alas, cannot be visited. The Vicomtes of Limoges built it in the eleventh and twelfth centuries to ward off the Counts of Périgord. Even Richard Coeur de Lion failed three times in 1182 to take it, but the English did grab it in 1356 in the Hundred Years War. Bertrand Du Guesclin took it back. A Breton, who had switched to fighting for Brittany's enemy France, Du Guesclin defeated the English on several occasions but was twice captured by them – once by the Black Prince. The English seem to have liked him, because while he was waiting for his ransom to be paid he was allowed to live at court in London.

The Protestants took the château during the Wars of Religion, but it was returned to Henri III of France. He was so short of money that, in 1582, he sold it to François de Cars, who built a fine Renaissance home out of the medieval fortress. Later the Talleyrand family owned it and removed most of its furniture and statues, even chimneys, to their Chalais Château. Last century they started to carry out repairs overdue since the eighteenth century.

Excideuil holds a lively market on Thursday around the fountain given to the town by a local man – Marshal Thomas Bugeaud, who helped to conquer Algeria and Morocco. After independence, Algeria sent back a statue that had been erected to him in Algiers. From the town ramparts there are lovely views.

Near St Médard-d'Excideuil, 2km NE, the writer André Maurois lived at Château d'Essendiéras after the First World War. His real name was André Herzog but during the war he preferred to write under a more French name. He shared a tent, rations and bathtub for six months with a British officer who during all that time never once asked him about his personal life. Maurois so admired this British reticence that he wrote a novel about it, *The Silences of Colonel Bramble*, which was an immediate bestseller in both France and England. He advised French people, 'If you have crossed the Atlantic alone in a small boat, say to an Englishman that you do a little sailing.' Times seem to have changed! He also wrote biographies of Queen Victoria, Edward VII, Disraeli, the poet Shelley (the superb book *Ariel*), Byron, the actress Mrs Siddons, the Imperialist Cecil Rhodes and the discoverer of penicillin, Sir Alexander Fleming. He worked tirelessly to bring the English and French together.

He wrote, too, about the Périgord countryside and food. He died in 1967.

MARKET Thursday (includes truffles in season)

HOTEL

Fin Chapon, place Château (53.62.42.38). Dates from 1750; still popular with locals for *confits* and Perigordian dishes. ROOMS B–C. MEALS A–E. Shut 15 December–31 January; Sunday evening, Monday low season.

EYMET
[DORDOGNE]

An old bastide and bustling market town on the river Drot at the extreme SW tip of Dordogne on the D933 SW of Bergerac, it becomes especially lively on Thursday, market day, when the local country people meet in the place des Arcades around the seventeenth-century fountain.

Despite destruction in wars it has rebuilt old houses and kept its arcades and its original half-timbered market-hall with a red-tiled roof and a second storey reached by a wooden staircase. Its fine fourteenth-century château has a small museum of local history and prehistory.

The market has fine fruit (especially plums) and vegetables, and the town is known for tinned *foie gras* and other conserves such as *confit* from six surrounding factories. Once it was known for pearl funeral wreaths!

TOURIST INFORMATION Château (53.23.81.60)

MARKET Thursday

HOTEL

Château, rue du Couvent (53.23.81.35). Extremely cheap, simple. ROOMS A. MEALS A–C. Shut 15–30 November.

RESTAURANT

Bastide, place Gambetta (53.23.71.37). Taste local conserves here. MEALS B–F. Shut 15 January–15 February; Sunday evening, Monday in winter.

LES EYZIES
[*See* Sites, page 59]

FAYRAC, CHÂTEAU
[DORDOGNE]

Just downstream from Castelnaud (*see* page 100), facing Beynac (*see* page 84), it was under the control of the lords of Castelnaud and was really a fortified manor house. The side facing Beynac has two massive round towers with pepper-pot roofs. The south side has a drawbridge over a double moat and a gate in battlemented walls but inside the courtyard it looks more like an old house, with a terrace overlooking the Dordogne river. It was built in the fourteenth century and altered up until the seventeenth century. Last century it was well restored. Fayrac looks quite pretty after the ferocity of Beynac. It is not open to the public, but attractive to view from the outside.

FÉNELON, CHÂTEAU DE
[DORDOGNE]

On the D50 which runs along the left bank of the Dordogne river, SE of Sarlat, near the village of Ste Mondane, is Château de Fénelon. It was built for war from the thirteenth to fifteenth centuries, standing on a succession of rocky terraces, with three lines of defences, fortified doorways and outer walls flanked by defence towers. It seems an unlikely setting for the birth, in 1651, of Fénelon, the writer, priest and finally Archbishop of Cambrai. But to be fair, by then the entrance façade had been made more home-like and a pleasant horseshoe staircase built in the courtyard.

Fénelon was the pen-name of François de Salignac de la Mothe-Fénelon, whose family had owned the château since it was built. He was one of eleven children. After the death of his uncle, whilst still a very young man, he took over as commendatory prior at Carennac in Lot, which meant that he got paid but did not have to do the job. However he did, and while there wrote *Télémaque*, the adventures of Ulysses' son. He did not publish it, however, until he was made tutor to Louis XIV's son. Then he made it into a tract for the boy's education. Louis XIV thought that it was a satire on his court and was extremely angry. One of Fénelon's ancestors was French Ambassador to Queen Elizabeth I of England.

The castle was beautifully restored by the Maleville family and I was lucky enough to see all over it. Now visits are guided and naturally very limited because the owners live there. There is a small Fénelon museum and a splendid little collection of vintage cars. The chapel is also open to the public.

As you walk up from Ste Mondane through woods you can at first see the château, then suddenly it is hidden behind its huge defence walls.

GIMEL-LES-CASCADES
[Corrèze]

A small village 12km NE of Tulle, it stands in a spectacular setting in the Corrèze valley. The river Montane flows through a wild, rock ravine and hurtles down a series of waterfalls for 140 metres.

A path marked with arrows from the village leads across Vuillier park to the best places to see the falls. The first fall, Grand Cascade, drops 45 metres and almost immediately the river falls another 27 metres (Redole Fall). The third fall, Queue de Cheval (Horse's Tail) pours from a little spur among the rocks, falling 60 metres into impassable ravines called Gouffre de l'Inferno (Gulf of Hell). The walk around the falls is tiring. The park is open March to November.

The church at Gimel has some remarkable treasures which you can see by request at the presbytery. They include a twelfth-century shrine of St Stephen with Limoges enamel and figures with eyes made of precious stones.

2km N is Étang de Ruffaud, a lagoon with bathing in a lovely setting of pines, birches and oaks.

HOTEL

Hostellerie La Vallée (55.21.40.60). Logis de France with good cooking. ROOMS C–E. MEALS B–E. Shut January; Sunday evening in winter.

GRAND BRASSAC
[Dordogne]

Village with a fine fortified church just N of Montagrier, it is on D103 running N of the D710 Périgueux–Ribérac road. The church has led a lively life. It was built in the twelfth century with one dome but from then on fortifications were added so that it could be used as a refuge in wars. A massive fortified belltower was added, and two more domes, defensive galleries, crenellations and narrow openings for shooting through. In the

Grand Brassac

belltower you can see where refugees climbed in. The Protestants knocked down part of it, but in 1599 it was repaired and
given a new apse. It is quite a unified building considering all the
additions. Statues and decorations inside are interesting.

GROLÉJAC
[DORDOGNE]

What a pity they couldn't have built a more pleasant bridge!
Apart from the approach bridge over the Dordogne, Groléjac,
set back on either side of the D704, 12km S of Sarlat, is a
charming village, geared for holidays, with hotels, swimming
and a good campsite (Les Granges, tel. 53.28.11.15).

On one side of the main road are narrow medieval streets
leading up to a Romanesque church with a flat stone roof and
embossed leather panelling inside. Adjacent is a fine classical
manor house. Along the road towards Gourdon are troglodyte
caves in the cliffs – the prehistoric site of La Gave.

HOTEL
Grillardin (53.28.11.02). Logis de France recommended for its
cooking. ROOMS B–C. MEALS A–D. Open 1 March–15 October.

HAUTEFORT
[DORDOGNE]

It was devastating to learn, in 1968, that the Château de
Hautefort had been 'burnt out'. The fire was caused by a discar-
ded cigarette end. Not only was it a lovely and historic château,
but seeking it years before had led us to this beautiful corner of
Dordogne where to this day some of the hamlets seldom see a
stranger. Blessedly, over the years since, the brave owner, Bar-
oness de Bastard, has restored it and now lives there.

Hautefort itself is just off the D704, SE of Excideuil, but
even this fairly busy main road is very attractive here, and the
side lanes lead to beautiful places.

Château de Hautefort is incredibly impressive. It stands
high above the countryside and you can see its yellow walls and
dark slate roof for miles. This building was made between 1640
and 1680. The drawbridge over which you enter, decorated with
flowers, is all that remains of the twelfth-century château of the
de Born family. Beyond the drawbridge is a courtyard with

Château de Hautefort

living rooms on three sides and the fourth open to the village beneath the castle walls.

The domed east tower contains a chapel with an altar from the coronation at Reims in 1824 of Charles X (1757–1836), the man who tried, after the defeat of Napoleon, to return France to a dictatorial monarchy and was forced to abdicate. The west tower, which contains a museum of the novelist Eugène Le Roy, has a fine chestnut timber dome, happily untouched by the fire.

The tapestry room in the château has lovely Flanders and Brussels tapestries. There are tenth-century vaults from the very earliest château here and an ancient parapet walk.

A great delight is to walk through the beautiful 30-hectare park to the terraces, from which the views are quite lovely.

Its most colourful owner in the mid-twelfth century was the troubadour Bertrand de Born, whose songs of love and war stirred up so much trouble for himself and all around him that Dante, in his *Divine Comedy*, put him in Hell for setting son against father. The father was the Plantagenet Henry II of England, his son the 'Young King' Henry Courtmantel.

Bertrand was a frequent guest of the intelligent, attractive and wayward Eleanor of Aquitaine, Henry II's wife, whose delight in the company of troubadours got her into trouble with her husband. Bertrand wrote pointedly satirical songs which caused havoc among the Plantagenet family.

When he and his brother Constantin were fighting over Château de Hautefort, Bertrand had the help of Henry Courtmantel, so Constantin called in Henry's younger brother Richard Coeur de Lion, and eventually they took it. But Bertrand persuaded old Henry II to give him back the château. Then, when he was away singing his songs, Constantin returned and destroyed it. Bertrand gave in and became a monk.

In the fifteenth century the Hautefort family took over, and in the seventeenth century Jean de Hautefort, Chamberlain to Louis XII, started to transform the feudal building. Jacques François de Hautefort, whose sister Marie was lady-in-waiting to the French Queen Anne of Austria, employed famous architects to rebuild the château and it has changed little since. Two of its owners went to the guillotine in the Revolution but it escaped destruction because it was used for a prison.

The Hauteforts' parish church was built by Jacques François as a hospital.

Marie de Hautefort, who was very pretty, caught the eye of the King Louis XIII but she found him too boring to become his mistress and married one of his generals instead.

Eugène Le Roy was born in the château in 1836, son of the steward and a seamstress. After overseas army service, he became a tax-collector in Domme and Montignac, and his experiences gave him a real understanding of peasant poverty. His best known novel, *Jacquou le Croquant*, was typical – peasants were his heroes, landowners his villains (*see* Rouffignac, page 156).

You can visit much of the château and its grounds (open daily Easter to early November; Sunday afternoons rest of the year).

MARKET First Monday of each month

L'HERM, CHÂTEAU
[*See* Rouffignac, page 156]

ISSAC
[Dordogne]

On the Crempse river 7½km E of Mussidan, which is on the N89, this is a village dominated by the superb Château de Mont-Réal, perched just westward on a great rock above an old road from Bergerac. One of its owners was Claude de Pontbriand, who went with Jacques Cartier on his second visit to Canada, gave the name Montréal to a rocky height on the St Lawrence river, saying that the river came second only to his own river Crempse!

The château still has some of its eleventh-century double ramparts. Half of the buildings are strong, bulky and medieval, with curtain walls and a round tower, the other half consist of a Renaissance house with attractive windows, columns and decorative medallions.

In a tower is a spiral staircase leading to a family chapel containing stone statues and the fifteenth-century tomb of the man who made it, François de Pontbriand, and one of his three wives. The chapel also contains the Holy Thorn carried by Sir John Talbot, commander of the English Army at the Battle of Castillon. Alas, it brought him no luck. His horse fell on him and a Frenchman chopped off his head with an axe while he lay helpless. Furthermore, the English lost the battle and lost Aquitaine.

ISSIGEAC
[Dordogne]

A delightful small town SE of Monbazillac vineyards, where the D14 crosses the Bahège river. It still has medieval overhanging timber-framed houses and a few Gothic mansions in its twisting streets. The Bishops of Sarlat used it as a holiday escape.

Issigeac

Around 1500, Bishop Armand de Gontaut-Biron built the church – Gothic, buttressed and with an octagonal belfry. The Protestants burned it but the local people rebuilt it. In 1699, Bishop François de Salignac, Fénelon's uncle, built Château des Évêques, a vast, strangely sombre but elegant palace flanked by square brick towers topped with turrets. It is now the town hall.

The Ancienne Prévote, a sixteenth-century courthouse, is flanked by two large pavilions with roofs the shape of a hull of an upturned ship.

Issigeac is prosperous and pleasant, its livelihood consisting of wine, fruit-growing (especially plums) and cereals.

MARKET Sunday

HOTEL

Bastides, Restaurant La Brucelière, place Capelle (53.78.72.28). A few attractive rooms. Excellent-value meals. Flowery terrace. ROOMS C–F. MEALS A–F. Shut November, February; Sunday evening, Monday except July, August.

JAVERLHAC ET LA CHAPELLE-ST-ROBERT
[DORDOGNE]

Another of the neglected villages in NW Dordogne, it is situated on an attractive stretch of the D75 between Nontron and Angoulême. Now a peaceful place, known for fishing in the unpolluted river Bandiat, it was an armaments town when charcoal from oaks was used for making iron; just like those old 'armament villages' of Lamberhurst and Horsmonden in Kent! Remains of the old forges are on the riverbank. The one at La Chapelle-St-Robert supplied the naval base at Rochefort. Small factories now make sandals. The sixteenth-century château is imposing, its great house forming a square flanked by a massive round tower with a pointed cap and another polygonal tower. The village has good cafés and restaurants with rooms.

The nearby abbey church dedicated to St Robert (one of the abbots) is simple but lovely. It was founded by Benedictines from the Auvergne on land given to them by a rich merchant. It has a huge, almost overpowering two-storey belltower watching over the hamlet of La Chapelle-St-Robert.

TOURIST INFORMATION Town Hall (53.56.30.18)
MARKET Second Monday in each month– fair

HOTEL

Tilleuls (53.56.30.12). Simple rooms. Logis de France. Excellent-value meals. ROOMS B. MEALS A–C.

JUMILHAC-LE-GRAND
[DORDOGNE]

The great château of Jumilhac-le-Grand is the most unusual in
Dordogne and a monument to the success of an arms manu-
facturer.

It stands on the D78, a very attractive road which runs NE
from the N21 from just above Thiviers, and it was built originally in the thirteenth century by the Knights Templars on a
jutting rock overlooking gorges of the river Isle. In 1579 it was
given by Henri IV to the Chapelle family, local ironmasters and
arms makers to whom he had good reason to be grateful. They
had not only made the cannons that he had used so successfully,
but also had lent him money. Antoine Chapelle immediately
started to add to it in a truly big way. Over the years the family
added a forest of pointed and pepper-pot turrets and towers
with highly ornamented Renaissance dormer windows until it
was like a castle from a fairy-tale, a genuine extravaganza in
ochre, grey, amber and red. They topped the towers with
forged-iron birds, angels, cupid, sun and moon.

Antoine Chapelle, like so many successful manufacturers
since, was not content with his new property and his fortune. He
wanted honours, too. He married a second wife, Marguerite de
Vars Coignac, a local heiress, and two years later bought another
seigneurie but he remained a commoner. Joining the nobility was
not just a matter of money then. He continued to serve Henri
and, in 1589, his cannons played a very important part in the
King's famous victory at Arques near Dieppe when, with 7000
men, Henri defeated 30,000 troops of the Catholic League commanded by the Duke of Mayenne. Henri finally made Jumilhac
a marquisate to make the Chapelles members of the nobility.

In the seventeenth century Antoine II of Jumilhac married
Louise de Hautefort, and a story worthy of a princess in the
tower, combined with a sex-triangle farce, came to the château.
Louise was not a faithful wife and her angry husband shut her in
a room in the castle where she spent her days spinning, painting
the walls and making love to her boyfriend who was summoned
by messages hung down from woollen thread which she had
spun and who got in disguised as a shepherd bringing her more

wool! Furthermore, she is said to have worn a big lacy pinafore, big enough to hide her lover in emergencies. You can see her room – La Chambre de la Fileuse – on visits. Antoine II's descendants by his second wife built the two side wings in the seventeenth century. They end in rectangular towers. An arcaded gallery encloses the courtyard. The right wing has a majestic stone staircase leading to a vast salon, with panelled walls and a marquetry floor said to be copied from one at Versailles. The left wing is not open to the public, but you can see an elaborately carved Louis XIII chimney piece with sculptures of the Four Seasons. The château is open daily 1 July to 15 September, Sunday afternoons and holidays 15 September to 15 November and 15 March to 1 July. It looks even more like a fairy-tale castle when floodlit in summer.

During the eighteenth century two of the Marquises were Generals in the French Royal Army. At the Revolution, Antoine Pierre, the current Marquis, was arrested but released, and he fled abroad. He returned to fight for Napoleon and died, in 1826, on army service for the restored monarchy. The château was sold to another munitions maker named Ouvrard. It changed hands and deteriorated but, in 1964, was bought by a descendant of the Chapelles, Comte Odil de Jumilhac, who restored it and now lives there.

The old family chapel beside the castle is now the village church. Eugène Le Roy, the rebellious novelist born in the Château de Hautefort (*see* page 123), was a tax-collector at Jumilhac-le-Grand and scandalized the authorities by seducing a girl, Marie Peyronnet, in the post office. This, and his anti-clerical and Republican views, got him the sack. He married Marie, defended his views in magazine articles and was finally reinstated. He died at Montignac in 1907.

Jumilhac has a huge market square.

MARKET Second and fourth Saturday of each month

LALINDE
[DORDOGNE]

A very lively little market town on the right bank of the Dordogne where a convenient bridge crosses from the pretty D29 road along the left bank. It is only 3km E of the main D660 road to Bergerac. The town was built between the river and the Lalinde canal, a life-saving link in the last days of river-borne transport.

From Mauzac, 7km upriver, there is a sharp drop in the water level and there was a very dangerous 100 metres of rapids called Saut de Gratusse where the boatmen used to need pilots. Despite this, many boats, cargoes and men were lost. At last, in the 1840s, the Canal de Lalinde was built to bypass the rapids. Ironically, 'the iron horse', the railway, was on its way within a few years, putting the boats out of business.

Lalinde was founded in 1267 as a bastide for the English by Jean de la Linde. Its bastide grid-pattern survives, despite great damage in wars over centuries. The Germans finished off the damage by burning it down in a huff when they were retreating in 1944 and being hurried on their way by French Resistance fighters. But fine old houses survive, many half-timbered. In the market-place is a stone cross marked 1351 and the old governor's house, dated 1597. A formidable little thirteenth-century fortress with pointed turrets overlooking the Dordogne is now the 'Château' hotel.

There are views over the Dordogne to the superb Cingle de Trémolat (see Trémolat, page 179) from the public gardens, and pleasant tree-shaded walks by the canal. A sailing, windsurfing and canoeing centre is alongside the swimming-pool and the campsite. Both the river and the canal are 'très poissoneux' – rich in fish.

The main crossing of the Dordogne by D660 is 3km W at Port-de-Couze (see Couze-et-St-Front, page 111). Opposite the bridge at Lalinde is St Front Chapel (twelfth century).

TOURIST INFORMATION Syndicat d'Initiative
(53.61.08.55)
MARKET Thursday; second Tuesday of each month –
fair

HOTELS

Château, 1 rue Verdun (53.61.01.82). *See* text. Fine terrace over river. Good value. In town centre but quiet. ROOMS C–D. MEALS C–F. Open 1 March–15 November. Shut Friday except July, August.

Forge, place Victor-Hugo (53.24.92.24). Old building in central square; also studios with kitchenette 3km away in grounds with river bathing, fishing. ROOMS D–E. MEALS A–G. Shut 1–7 October; 22 December–31 January; Sunday evening in winter.

RESTAURANT

Relais St Jacques, place Église at St Capraise-de-Lalinde 4km W (53.23.22.14). Wonderful value for excellent Perigordian cooking. MEALS A–F. Shut 1–16 April; 1–15 December.

LAMONZIE-MONTASTRUC
[DORDOGNE]

Just off N21 NE of Bergerac, Montastruc is a fine classical seventeenth-century château on a rock, with towers at each corner.

LAMOTHE MONTRAVEL
[DORDOGNE]

At the far W of Dordogne almost into the St Émilion vineyards, Lamothe Montravel is close to Castillon where the defeat of General John Talbot, Earl of Shrewsbury, by the French in 1453 marked the end of the Hundred Years War (*see* History and Art, page 33). A monument S of D936, W of Lamothe, shows the spot where Talbot was killed by an axe. At least he still has a fine Bordeaux Grand Cru wine named after him.

Montravel wine is really part of the Bordeaux wine enclave but cannot be classified as Bordeaux because it is in Dordogne. Montravel AOC white wines are dry, *demi-sec* or sweet, light with soft fruit. Red wine is sold under the appellation of Bergerac. Côtes de Montravel from hillside vineyards is sweet, made from Sémillon, Sauvignon and Muscadelle grapes, and is very like the best sweet Premières Côtes de Bordeaux.

LANQUAIS, CHÂTEAU DE
[Dordogne]

Lanquais is a tiny market village filled with old buildings just S of the Dordogne SW of the Port de Couze bridge and 20km E of Bergerac. The remarkable grandiose château is a fifteenth-century fort, with a huge tower and a lovely Renaissance palace clamped on it. The feudal half has slits for defensive firing; the palace has beautiful decorated windows. It is fully furnished with seventeenth-century pieces, Italianate chimneys and painted ceilings (open 1 April to 31 October daily except Tuesday).

LARCHE
[Corrèze]

Attractive village on the N89 W of Brive, beside the Vézère river. The D119 and D60 SE and SW from here are lovely roads through beautiful scenery.

HOTEL
Glycines (55.85.30.12). Used by locals. ROOMS D–C. MEALS A–D. Shut 15 December–15 January.

LE LARDIN-ST-LAZARE
[Dordogne]

Village on the N89 originally known for glass production; now produces paper. The D704 SW leads to Montignac (*see* page 144). Château Peyraux, medieval with a fifteenth-century tower, is 1km N. One of the Royère family who lived there brought back Arab horses from the Crusades, introducing the breed to France.

HOTEL

Sautet, route de Montignac (53.51.27.22). Family-run hotel, flower garden, swimming-pool. ROOMS D–E. MEALS C–G. Shut 20 December–15 January; Sunday in winter, Saturday lunch in summer.

LIMEUIL
[Dordogne]

This little beauty spot climbs up a cliffside from a quay on the Dordogne river to the attractive little D31 road which joins Trémolat to Le Bugue. Here at Limeuil the river Vézère joins the Dordogne, with a handsome bridge Pont Coude (Elbow Bridge), spanning both rivers. Old houses are tightly packed in winding streets up the cliffside and from the esplanade of the old castle is a huge panoramic view over the rivers which both loop like serpents. The domed Chapel of St Martin on the quayside, now being restored, was built in 1194 during the English occupation, and dedicated to St Thomas à Becket, the Archbishop of Canterbury murdered on the steps of his cathedral. Richard Coeur de Lion was one of its founders. Until the 1850s, the villagers made boats and weaved cloth. Now the village is a favourite with tourists for its beautiful position and for excellent coarse fishing, canoeing and swimming.

HOTEL

Beauregard, Restaurant Les Terraces, route de Trémolat

Limeuil

(53.22.03.15). In the country outside Limeuil, used by local people. Good cooking. ROOMS D–E. MEALS B–G. Shut 30 September–20 May. Restaurant shut for lunch on Tuesday and Friday.

LISLE
[Dordogne]

Very pleasant small town hidden away on the D78, 16km by minor roads NW from Périgueux. Lisle has made good use of the river Dronne which runs at the end of the town to entice campers and others who want a hideaway for swimming and trout fishing. It has a four-day fête in the middle of August and a lively useful market known for fresh poultry and walnuts in season. The Romanesque and Gothic church restored in the sixteenth century is charming. The D78 is a pretty road and Bourdeilles is only 8km NE.

MARKET Wednesday (sometimes Tuesday, so check)
FESTIVALS Four days around third Sunday in August –
fête

MAREUIL-SUR-BELLE
[Dordogne]

Mareuil has been on the route to Angoulême since Roman soldiers marched this way. It became one of the four great baronies of Périgord. Now it is a link-town on the D939 between Périgueux and Angoulême for commerce and tourism, only 6km from the Dordogne–Charente border.

Its proud château, heavily defended by deep moats and ramparts flanked at the corners by horseshoe towers, was built in the sixteenth century after a twelfth-century castle had been partly destroyed in the Wars of Religion. It was actually abandoned in 1770, and suffered in the Revolution and by neglect afterwards. Since 1965 it has been carefully restored as home for the Duke and Duchess of Montebello. A section of the moat remains fed by the little river Belle. You enter up a ramp to the fortified gate defended by two towers. In one of them is a Flamboyant Gothic chapel – a little gem. You can visit rooms with Louis XV furniture, gardens, the keep and underground prisons (open afternoons Easter to 31 October except Wednesday; just Sunday afternoon rest of the year).

Mareuil is surrounded by châteaux. Most are closed to the public but are worth seeing from the outside. Beaulieu, near the Ribérac road, the D708, is 3km away. Beauregard is 3km away, along a path running left from the Ribérac road. Château Repaire is 2km along a tiny road left off the D708. They are all marked on the yellow Michelin map.

Vieux-Mareuil, 5km towards Brantôme on the D939, has a thirteenth-century fortified church.

HOTEL

Étang Bleu at Vieux-Mareuil, (53.60.92.63). 2km N by D93. In gardens and a park by a lake. You can eat on the terrace in summer. Good-value meals. ROOMS E. MEALS A–G. Shut 2 January–31 March; Sunday evening, Monday in winter.

MASSERET
[CORRÈZE]

Village on the N20 as it leaves Corrèze into Haute-Vienne, making for Limoges. It is in attractive wooded country. In the village centre is a modern tower with a viewing table – 104 steps up! It is worth climbing to see a beautiful panorama all round you. Ambazec Hills are to the north, to the east you can see Millevaches Plateau, Monédières Massif and, on a clear day, the Auvergne Mountains.

TOURS DE MERLE
[CORRÈZE]

The Maronne valley SE of Argentat is beautiful wild country. Follow the small roads on the yellow Michelin map to Tours de Merle, a remarkable ruined fortress with towers standing like gaunt sentries on a rock almost surrounded by a bend in the river. In the Middle Ages this was the impregnable lair of the Lords of Merle, who were the most feared in the region. The first castle was built in the eleventh century and over generations younger sons built their own castles alongside until there were seven by the fourteenth century. The great rock was impregnable even to armies and it was the one stronghold in the Auvergne and Bas-Limousin that the English failed to take in the Hundred Years War.

You can see it best by taking the attractive little D13 off N120 and approaching from the S through Goules and over the river by a suspension bridge, climbing the hillside opposite. There is a car-park approximately 700 metres beyond the bridge. You have a lovely view from the hilltop of the castle ruins and the ancient houses at the foot. A *son et lumière* is held each evening from mid-July to mid-September (times vary; tel. 55.28.24.35).

MEYMAC
[CORRÈZE]

Little town at the southern end of the Millevaches Plateau below Mont Bessou (984 metres). You can reach it from the N89 Brive-Tulle-Ussel road by the D36 or D979 (8 to 9km) and it is an attractive starting point for exploring the plateau. Built around a former abbey, it has fine old houses with pointed slate-covered roofs round the Romanesque church and an old covered market with a wooden frame on granite pillars. Pilgrims still come to see the twelfth-century black Virgin on a pillar in the church.

TOURIST INFORMATION place de la Fontaine
(55.95.18.43)

HOTEL

Splendid, 76 ave Limousine (55.95.12.11). Who could resist a Logis with a name like this and two 'chimneys' for good local cuisine and service? Simple rooms. ROOMS A–C. MEALS A–D. Shut 1–31 December; Sunday.

MEYSSAC
[CORRÈZE]

Old village 2km along D38 E of Collonges-la-Rouge (*see* page 108) and built of the same red sandstone. The red earth is known as Collonges clay and is still used for making pottery. Lovely old houses and towers make the streets of Meyssac very attractive. You can visit pottery workshops. D38 is a pleasant road all the way to Brive.

MILANDES, CHÂTEAU DES
[DORDOGNE]

The riverside road from Castelnaud and Fayrac continues westward to a different type of château. In 1478, François de Caumont, Lord of Castelnaud, had Milandes built – a delightful Renaissance château with terraces and gardens to the river – as a wedding present for his wife. The Caumont family lived there until the Revolution, which it happily survived.

In the 1930s '*La Perle Noire*' of Paris cabaret, Josephine Baker, the slum child from St Louis, Missouri, who was Queen of the *Folies Bergère* by the age of twenty, was being driven around the Dordogne in her Bugatti Royale, saw this run-down château and fell in love with it.

When the Second World War started in 1939, the US was not yet involved so she stayed in France. When the Germans took Paris, she went to Les Milandes. There she risked her life hiding RAF and Polish aircrew. Then she worked with the Resistance, for which she was given the Legion of Honour and rosette by de Gaulle.

After the war, she bought Les Milandes, married her agent Joe Bouillon, and they both worked hard in show business to make the money to restore the château and park. Then she tried to make a dream come true. She adopted orphan children from around the world, all of different races, colour and creeds, to show the unity of the human race.

She housed and gave jobs to seventy local people. But she

could not afford it all. She even opened a gambling casino in the grounds to help pay expenses, but few people came. Joe, driven to despair by her financial incompetence, left her. Just before the whole scheme collapsed, we were taken to tea with her. Josephine opened champagne, played the gramophone and danced. None of us knew that she was near to bankruptcy. She went down in style. Her dream ended in 1964. Some of her furniture and effects are still in the château, with possessions of the Caumont family. The carvings are magnificent. The park and garden are beautifully kept (open daily Palm Sunday to early October).

MOLIÈRES
[DORDOGNE]

English bastide W of Cadouin (*see* page 96), begun in the thirteenth century but never finished. This is a delightful village but can be windswept. Guillaume de Toulouse was ordered to build it for the English King but could not raise enough money in the City of London where the bankers complained that it was too expensive and not needed. It has a fine Gothic church with a tall square defensive tower. Old houses with arcades remain in the square where little local markets are held.

MONBAZILLAC
[DORDOGNE]

Château de Monbazillac, S of Bergerac, is one of my favourite castles, for it is not only very beautiful but also in lovely scenery, with magnificent views from its terrace. Also, its wine is one of the most underestimated in France, if you keep it long enough – sweet, but amber gold, and richer than Sauternes. Drink it very cold as an aperitif, with pâté or desserts. I have converted people who hate sweet wines by serving them a ten-year-old Monbazillac with strawberries. At one time it was sold as Sauternes.

Follow signposts S of Bergerac on the pretty D13 road W of the N21. You climb to the medieval hamlet of Monbazillac among vineyard-covered hillsides and come to the main gate in the curtain wall. The château inside is of grey stone with attractive brown roofs and round towers at each corner. Although with battlements, it was built in 1550 by François d'Aydie, Viscount of Ribérac, as much as a home as for defence. However, it became a Protestant stronghold in the Wars of Religion. One of the rooms is devoted to the history of Protestantism in the area, with portraits of Luther, Calvin, Hus and Cranmer and Bibles and prayer books, many printed in Holland. The Dutch connection started in the thirteenth century when Monbazillac and Bergerac wines were exported to Holland. When Protestants fled to Holland and England after the Edict of Nantes was revoked and Protestatism became illegal, the flow of wine to Holland became greater. Other rooms are devoted to various crafts, to Perigordian furniture and to a history of the area.

The château is owned by the Wine Co-operative of Monbazillac, who have restored it. The cellars, which run the full length and breadth of the château, are laid out as a museum of ancient bottles and winemaking equipment. In the square you can taste and buy the wine, but I would recommend the Co-operative Cave down on the D933, where they will give you a half-hour tour showing the very modern methods of vinification, then a tasting in the seventeenth-century *chais*. They also make Pécharmant from Château La Renaudie N of Bergerac, Bergerac white, red and rosé, a *pétillant* (gently sparkling) white called Festival made from pure grape juice by the Champagne method. You can buy wine here and take a meal in a restaurant.

Signposted along a tiny lane S from the château is the hamlet of Colombier, which you can also reach signposted along another tiny lane from the N21. Here is Château de la Jaubertie, where Nicholas Ryman makes what most drinkers believe to be the best Bergerac white wines and very good reds by modern methods (*see* Wine, page 23). He bought the truly charming sixteenth-century château with the vineyards when he sold his stationery empire in Britain and it is worth visiting the caves, if only to see his home. Henri of Navarre, later Henri IV of

France, who loved women, wine, food and life, gave it to his mistress Gabrielle d'Estrées and her initials are still carved on it. Alas, you cannot go inside but it looks delightful from the gates with its garden and lawns in front of an elegant house. You *can*, however, taste the wines.

HOTELS

La Diligence, route Eymet D933 (53.58.30.48). Modernized old inn with magnificent terrace views over vineyards. ROOMS D–E. MEALS C–G. Shut part February; 15–30 June; Tuesday evening, Wednesday except in summer.

Château Rauly-Saulieut, 5km W over D933 on D14 (53.63.35.31). Nineteenth-century manor house in a park with good views of vineyards; swimming-pool. Expensive, but some good cheaper menus. ROOMS G. MEALS C–G. Open 1 March–10 November. Restaurant shut Sunday evening, Monday, 15 September–15 June.

Voyageurs, at Bouniagues on N21, 2km past Colombier (53.58.32.26). Good cheap Logis. ROOMS A–D. MEALS A–E. Shut 15 October–15 November; Sunday evening, Monday in winter.

RESTAURANT

Closerie St-Jacques, la Bourg (53.58.37.77). Large old house. Excellent but pricey meals. MEALS E–G. Shut 2 January–early February; Sunday evening, Monday in winter.

MONPAZIER
[DORDOGNE]

One of our favourite old towns. Beautiful bastide, built in 1284 for Edward I of England and little changed. The market square has its lovely old arcaded houses running round it, a covered market-hall with its old measures for grain, and, at a corner on one of many delightful side-streets, the thirteenth-century inn, the France, where I have eaten well for more than thirty years. The church is fortified, its nave is original from the thirteenth

Monpazier

century, the surrounds from the fifteenth century and the charming rose window from 1550. The thirteenth-century Maison de Chapitre at one corner of the square was used as a tithe barn.

Try to stay overnight in Monpazier, especially in mid-summer so that you can see it when the many day visitors, all seemingly taking pictures, have gone. It lies on the D660, 26km after it crosses the Dordogne E of Bergerac and continues SE. Another beautiful road, the D53, reaches it from the NE at Belvès on the D25.

Monpazier is a few km N of Château Biron (*see* page 87) and it was built under an agreement with Pierre de Gontaut, Seigneur of Biron. It changed hands and was pillaged by the French and English several times in the Hundred Years War. Its rival was the bastide of Villefranche-du-Périgord (*see* page 192) to the S (now on the D660). Unknown to each other, they each decided to raid and loot the other's town on the same night. They set off in the darkness taking different routes. Both raiding parties arrived home very pleased with themselves, loaded with loot, only to find that their own homes had been looted too. All they could do was to take back all the booty.

In the Wars of Religion Monpazier was taken by the Protestant leader Geoffroy de Vivans. As with Domme, the French guidebooks, including the *Michelin Green Guide*, accuse him of doing it 'by trickery'. In fact, he used his brains, saved both towns a lot of damage and in turn saving a lot of men's lives.

In 1637, Monpazier was the centre for the revolt of the poor peasants, who were starving under the burden of viciously high rents and church tithes. They were called Croquants after their main weapon, a bent pitchfork called a *cros*. A weaver called Buffarot led 8000 of these rebels through the countryside, attacking and plundering castles. They even took Bergerac. But the landowners and gentry closed ranks against them and the Governor of Aquitaine's troops captured Buffarot, who was broken on the wheel in Monpazier Square.

The peasants of Monpazier joined the Revolution but like many others in France their complaints were against the King, the landlords and the hierarchy of the Church, not against their religion or their own local clergy who were often as poor as them. To make the point, the people of Monpazier carved a declaration that the people of France believe in a Supreme Being and the Immortality of the Soul on the tympanum of their church door. It is still there.

TOURIST INFORMATION place Centrale (high season –
53.22.68.59)
MARKETS Thursday; Thursday and Sunday morning
October–December – Chestnut Fair

HOTEL

France, 21 rue St Jacques (53.22.60.06). Delightful old inn used by locals. In the thirteenth century it was an *auberge* of the Château Biron. Very simple rooms. True Perigordian cooking and nice atmosphere. ROOMS A–B. MEALS A–E. Shut Wednesday.

RESTAURANT

Bastide, 52 rue St Jacques (53.22.60.59). Popular with visitors

seeking local dishes. Cheapest menu is *very* cheap. MEALS A–E.
Shut 15 January–31 March; Monday.

MONTFERRAND-DU-PÉRIGORD
[DORDOGNE]

A very charming medieval village rising in terraces above the
river Couze just off the D2 between Cadouin and Monpazier. Its
sixteenth-century covered market on squat pillars, old houses
with dovecots, and Romanesque chapel make it a photogenic
scene. High above it are the ruins of its fifteenth-century
château, where monks hid from the Huguenots the holy shroud
of Cadouin (*see* page 96) which turned out to be a fake.

HOTEL
Lou Peyrol (53.22.33.63). Pleasant Logis de France with above-
average cooking. ROOMS B–D. MEALS A–F. Shut 30
September–31 March.

MONTFORT, CHÂTEAU
[DORDOGNE]

High on a rock falling sheer to the Dordogne's great Cingle de
Montfort, where the river sweeps in a horseshoe loop almost
meeting itself, Montfort is in the most picturesque setting of
almost all the Dordogne châteaux. It is impressive indeed, but
something of a mixture of styles from several centuries. Much of
it was rebuilt last century.

The man who rivalled Richelieu in his lust to destroy fine old
castles gave it its name – the Simon de Montfort who led the
Albigensian 'crusade', not his son who led the barons' revolt in
England. He destroyed the château completely in 1214 after
taking it from Bernard de Casnac. It was rebuilt by the Turenne
family, and taken by the English after sieges. Pons de Turenne
got it back. The family were Protestants in the Wars of Religion

and made it a stronghold. It was severely damaged several times as a result. You cannot visit it, but it is well worth seeing from the outside.

MONTIGNAC
[DORDOGNE]

Long before Lascaux Cave was discovered nearby in 1940 (*see* Sites, page 63) Montignac was an important market town. It is on the Vézère river, where the D704 from Lardin meets the D706. The town rises up the hillside, on terraces from riverside buildings left from the days of its river trade. The Counts of Périgord had a château here until the fourteenth century. The twelfth-century priory church was altered in the fourteenth and seventeenth centuries.

Eugène Le Roy (1836–1907), author of *Jacquou le Croquant*, lived for the last years of his life in rue 14-juillet. There is an exhibition in the Syndicat d'Initiative of his work.

TOURIST INFORMATION place Bertran-de-Born
(53.51.82.60)
MARKETS Wednesday, Saturday morning

HOTELS

Château de Puy Robert, 1½km by D65 along left bank of Vézère river (53.51.92.13). Little château of Napoleon III period now a Relais et Châteaux hotel. Elegantly decorated. Very expensive and very good. ROOMS G. MEALS F–G. Open early May–15 October.

Soleil d'Or, rue 4-Septembre (53.51.80.22). Fine house, quiet gardens, high-class Perigordian cooking. Swimming-pool. ROOMS D–E. MEALS C–G. Shut mid-January–28 February.

Lascaux, 109 ave Jean-Jaurès (53.51.82.81). Logis de France. Good value. ROOMS B–D. MEALS A–E. Shut 26 November–31 December; part February; Thursday evening, Saturday lunch, Sunday evening low season.

MONT-RÉAL, CHÂTEAU DE
[*See* Issac, page 124]

Château de Mont-Réal

NEUVIC
[Corrèze]

A place very much worth seeing if you are on a wandering holiday. A very attractive hillside village, it borders Neuvic Lake on the D982 between Ussel and the Gorges de Dordogne near Aigle, and has a beach with a sailing school, watersports centre and good fishing. From the hill behind, at 1625 metres, are magnificent panoramic views of the Monts Dore and Cantal.

The lake was originally called Lac de Triouzoune because it is fed from the N by the river Triouzoune, a tributary of the Dordogne. A massive dam, Neuvic d'Ussel (27 metres high and 145 metres long), holds the river to form the lake, giving a reservoir capacity of 5000 million gallons. The water is pumped to a power-station 5km away, S of Sérandon in the Dordogne valley. Then the waters of the Triouzoune flow on to the Aigle Dam. You can reach Neuvic d'Ussel Dam by a small lakeside road.

A road round the N of the lake leads to Puy de Manzagol. From the top is a remarkable view of the Neuvic Lake and the Massif Central.

W of Neuvic on the D991 approximately 12km in a wild setting on a rock above Luzège Gorges are the ruins of a romantic castle, Ventadour. Like so many medieval castles, it was believed to be impregnable. It fell to the English in the Hundred Years War – by treason, it is said. A famous troubadour, Bernard de Ventadour, was born in the castle, and inevitably he arrived at the court of Eleanor of Aquitaine, Queen of Troubadours, when she was Queen of France. However, when she married Henry Plantagenet he joined the court of the Count of Toulouse.

The viscounts deserted their uncomfortable castle when the Renaissance came to France from Italy and built themselves a lovely mansion in Ussel (*see* page 183).

There is a path to the ruins of Ventadour. They are worth seeing, if only for the awesome views of the Luzège Gorges through breaches in the walls. The gorges were called 'the moat of Ventadour'. Some moat! The Luzège river twists through steep sides. The best way to reach the ruins is from Moustier-Ventadour, a village just off the attractive D991. A narrow road takes you to within a 15-minute walk by the path.

TOURIST INFORMATION rue Poste, Neuvic (July, August – 55.95.88.78)
MARKET Tuesday

HOTEL

Lac, at Neuvic-Plage, 3km E (55.95.81.43). Logis de France. ROOMS E. MEALS C–E. Open 1 April–30 September.

NEUVIC-SUR-L'ISLE
[Dordogne]

Industrial town (this Neuvic manufactures shoes), just off N89 SW of Périgueux, which has a beautiful classic 'fairy-tale' château close by the river Isle in a fine park. Built in 1520–30 by the Marquis de Fayolle in early Renaissance style, it has mullioned windows, dormers in the roof and round towers with dunce's hats at each corner. An earlier château belonged to the Talleyrand-Périgord family, from which came Prince Talleyrand, aptly described as a cynical priest turned cynical politician who 'betrayed Napoleon to save France' and, as Ambassador to London, did a lot to further the cause of French cuisine in London with his banquets cooked by his great chef Carême.

MARKETS Tuesday, Saturday

NONTRON
[Dordogne]

Busy but unhurried town N of Brantôme on the D675 and the attractive D75 heading NW to Angoulême, it is popular with tourists for its old city and nearby rivers and *étangs* (lagoons) for fishing. It is in a deep valley of the little Bandiat river, overlooked by the old city standing on a rock above a ravine. The ramparts still look strong and impressive. The château, rebuilt in the eighteenth century, is in a superb position. It replaced one which had several famous owners, including Françoise de Bretagne, Vicomtesse de Limoges, Henri IV and the Pompadours. In the present château is a museum of dolls. Nontron used to be famous for wooden-handled knives.

A further 8km to the north is Étang de St Estèphe, main leisure centre for the people of Nontron – 75 acres of lake with a shady bank.

TOURIST INFORMATION 1 place Champ-de-Foire
(June–September – 53.56.00.53)
MARKETS Wednesday, Saturday
FAIR 18th of each month

FESTIVALS mid-August – fête

HOTEL

Grand, 3 place Agard (53.56.11.22). Traditional pleasant Logis; regional cooking. Range of menus. ROOMS B–E. MEALS A–F. Shut Sunday evening in winter.

OBJAT
[CORRÈZE]

Very important little market town on the D901 NW of Brive and 6km W of Le Saillant in the Gorges de Vézère. It is an agricultural market centre, especially for geese and other poultry, and for lamb. Markets are held daily in summer, and Wednesday, Friday and Sunday for the rest of the year. There is a big Lamb Fair in January (fourth Monday).

If you want to decide for yourself if the feeding of geese for *foie gras* and *confit* is cruel, you can go to Cofimil in avenue Coudert (55.84.13.33) to visit a farm where they raise and feed geese, and see there how conserves (*confit*) are produced, taste and buy.

MARKETS See text

HOTELS

Pré Fleuri, 1090 ave Jules Ferry (55.25.83.92). Only seven comfortable rooms, but building up a very good reputation for cooking, especially of local produce. ROOMS B–C. MEALS D–G. Shut 10–25 January; Monday off season.
France, ave Clemenceau (55.25.80.38). Logis. ROOMS A–C. MEALS A–E. Shut 20 September–10 October; 24 December–2 January; Sunday.

PAUNAT
[DORDOGNE]

In a nice valley just W of Limeuil, where the Vézère and Dordogne meet spectacularly, Paunat is a very pleasant hamlet 3km from the Dordogne. Like Trémolat, nearby on the river, it has a fortified church like a fort with a belltower – few windows, looking rather grim and more like a prison. No doubt both of them were needed in the troubled Middle Ages. It has a single nave inside – a bit like a warehouse. It was built in the twelfth century, and restored in the fifteenth. An abbey founded here in the sixth century was sacked by the Normans in 849 and rebuilt in 890 by the Bishop of Périgueux.

PÉRIGUEUX
[*See* Major Towns, page 45]

PLAZAC
[DORDOGNE]

A small town in a pretty valley of the Vimont river, where it joins the river Moustier, Plazac is reached along the very pleasant D45 from Thonac or from other little roads off the D706 between Les Eyzies and Montignac.

On a small hill stands a Romanesque church in an old churchyard surrounded by cypresses. The church has a curious twelfth-century belltower-keep roofed with lauze-stone – roughly hewn slabs of schiste slate. A chapel has sixteenth-century wall paintings.

The roads running into the valley have nice views of typical Périgord scenery. The route to the small town of Moustier, on the Vézère, cuts through forests of parasol pines, as though it had strayed from Provence.

The Château des Chabans nearby was built in the sixteenth and seventeenth centuries.

This is a lovely calm, peaceful area to explore. You can fish
for trout in the rivers or the small lake.

MARKET Third Thursday of each month

POMPADOUR, CHÂTEAU
[CORRÈZE]

This imposing fifteenth-century château is at Arnac-
Pompadour, 15km W of Uzerche. It had belonged to the
influential Pompadour family and took its place in history when,
in 1745, King Louis XV gave it to the leader of fashion at his
court, a Parisienne called Jeanne Antoinette Poisson, in order to
enoble her as the Marquise de Pompadour. She was his favourite
mistress from the moment he spotted her at a ball until she died,
in 1764. It is said that she never lived in her château. Perhaps
not, but a woman of her lively mind and love of theatre must
surely have at least been to see the gift which did so much to
improve her position and power.

Pompadour was a wit – sometimes a cruel wit. I have long
wondered if Louis XV was showing a wry sense of humour when
he turned her château into the royal stud in 1761. Last century it
became the nursery of the Anglo–Arab breed of horses and it
remains a very important stud and horse-racing venue. Much of
the original building was destroyed in the Revolution but it has
since been faithfully restored. Only the terraces and the stables
are open to the public. The château houses the stud staff and
their offices.

The château has a majestic façade with round towers and
square wings. The terrace is flanked by low towers and encircled
by a moat. Opposite is the stud where the famous Puy-Marmont
stallions live. There are about a hundred of many different
breeds but mostly Anglo–Arabs. It is open from 2 July to 28
February. Horse shows, jumping and race meetings are held in
summer.

Nearby is a Club Mediterranée devoted, of course, to riding.

The reason why Pompadour did not live in her château was
that she became too busy, not only keeping Louis happy with

love (assisted, she claimed, by stuffing herself with truffles) and private theatricals, but also running France's public affairs for him – disastrously. When Frederick the Great of Prussia lampooned her, she broke off the country's highly successful alliance with him and got France involved with Austria in the Seven Years War (1756–63) against Britain and Prussia. France was utterly defeated and lost most of its colonies in the West Indies and Canada. She also spent vast fortunes on her favourite interests and sent Louis bankrupt. But she did set up the École Militaire and the royal porcelain factory at Sèvres, and she spread the message of truffles as an aphrodisiac.

The village name is officially Arnac-Pompadour, but it is the château in which visitors are interested.

TOURIST INFORMATION Town Hall (55.73.30.43)
MARKETS Tuesday, Thursday, Saturday

HOTELS

Auberge de la Marquise, ave Ecuyers (55.73.33.98). Near the railway station. Good gastronomic dishes. ROOMS D–E. MEALS C–G. Shut 31 October–1 May; Tuesday low season.

Auberge de la Mandrie, 5km W by D7 (55.73.37.14). Not many village schools end up as hotels with swimming-pool and poolbar. Gardens. Regional cooking. ROOMS C. MEALS B–E.

Hippodrome, 26 ave Midi (55.73.35.03). 500m from château and race track. Regional cooking. ROOMS B–C. MEALS A–E. Shut Monday low season.

PUYGUILHEM, CHÂTEAU DE
[*See* Villars, page 190]

PUYMARTIN, CHÂTEAU
[DORDOGNE]

Attractive château on the D47, NW of Sarlat, which was the headquarters of the Catholic army sent to save Sarlat from the

Château de Puymartin

Protestants in the Wars of Religion. Built in the fifteenth and sixteenth centuries in golden stone with stone slate roofs, it has several wings linked by towers and defended by curtain-walls. It has been restored by the Beaux Arts department since the Second World War and is open for visits 1 July to 15 September. It looks peaceful now in its field setting, despite its old defence towers, and has some really delightful decorations and furnishings, including six Flemish tapestries showing scenes from the Trojan Wars, eighteenth-century Aubusson tapestries and wall paintings with mythological themes. The main hall has a fine chimney and a ceiling with beams painted in the seventeenth century. The former guardroom has fine tapestries, furniture and paintings. The oldest room is the hexagonal chapel. A pity that it is not open in earlier months. Perhaps they don't want to disturb the resident ghost – a 'white lady'.

QUEYSSAC-LES-VIGNES
[Corrèze]

Little village built on a spur among vineyards, woods and fields, SW of Beaulieu-sur-Dordogne. Part of the old castle has become a restaurant, Au Vin Paillé (taken from *vin de paille*, a local sweet wine made from grapes dried on a bed of straw). Go through the courtyard and you reach an old castle tower with a viewing table at the top. From here, you have a wonderful panorama of the Dordogne valley, and the Corrèze and Lot countryside to Castelnau Castle, Carennac, Turenne Castle, Vic Roc and St Laurent Tower, which is high above the charming little town of St Céré, and now houses a museum of the tapestries and ceramics of Jean Lurçat, the artist who made his home in the ancient tower.

RASTIGNAC, CHATEAU DE
[*See* La Bachellerie, page 77]

RIBÉRAC
[Dordogne]

The pretty D78 SW from Brantôme through Bourdeilles reaches Ribérac on the D708 and the river Dronne. It is the main centre for the villages of western Dordogne as far as the Double Forest, and, for Britons, a centre for *gîte* holidays in this still sparsely populated area. Some Britons have bought houses round here. It is a particularly important agricultural centre, with a weekly market, several fairs and a weekly walnut market from October to December.

A very pleasant little town of 4000 people on a slope covered in cypress trees, it has two interesting churches – one Romanesque (Faye), the other modern with a Byzantine look.

The troubadour-poet Arnaut Daniel was born here in a castle which has since disappeared. He was highly praised as a poet by Dante in the *Divine Comedy*. Inevitably, he went to Eleanor of Aquitaine's court.

Good campsite beside the river (La Dronne; tel. 53.90.50.08).

TOURIST INFORMATION place Gen-de-Gaulle (shut afternoons low season – 53.90.03.10)
MARKETS Friday; Wednesday, May–September – wicker basket market
FAIRS First Friday of July, August, September, October; third week in August – Annual Agricultural Fair; Wednesday, October–December – walnut market

HOTELS

France, rue M. Dufraisse (53.90.00.61). Good-value Logis. ROOMS B–D. MEALS A–F. Shut 5–27 January.
Mas de Montet, at Petit Bersac, 10km NW by D20 (53.90.08.71). seventeenth-century Renaissance manor in a park. Regional cooking. ROOMS F–G. MEALS C–G. Shut January; Tuesday.

RICHEMONT, CHÂTEAU DE
[DORDOGNE]

Built in 1550–80 by Pierre de Bourdeilles (the writer Brantôme and lay Abbot of Brantôme), N of Brantôme on D98. It is near the little village of St Crépin-de-Richemont close to the river Boulou.

It has two long wings at right angles and has an impressive square tower. Brantôme died there in 1614 and his tomb is in the decorated chapel. The château is open 15 July to 31 August, except Friday.

The next village, St Félix-de-Bourdeilles, is very attractive.

LA ROQUE-GAGEAC
[DORDOGNE]

This beautiful village on the D703 E from Beynac clings so precariously to a cliff above the Dordogne that you expect some of the houses to fall into the river. In the winter of 1956–7 some did just that, with people inside. Rocks still fall, occasionally killing people or destroying houses.

Houses of ochre stone are bunched at the bottom of the tall grey cliff beside the river, and steep alleyways climb between more old houses, under archways and past corners of rock to the holm-oaks and the upper terrace where there are magnificent views of the river from beside the humble twelfth-century church.

It was an important strategic post for centuries. The English failed to take it in the Hundred Years War. Then it was a small port for wine barges.

The sixteenth-century Manoir de Tarde at the foot of the rocks, flanked by a turret with a pepper-pot roof, was the home of a distinguished family. Canon Jean Tarde, born here about 1561, was a well-known humanist, mathematician and astronomer who knew Galilei Galileo. He left behind important records of Sarlat. One of his descendants, Gabriel de la Tarde, who lived in the Manoir until his death in 1904, was a well-known sociologist.

Château de la Marlartie at the west end of the village looks as if it is fifteenth century, but was built in the nineteenth century.

This stretch of river is popular for bathing, sunbathing and for fishing from gravel banks.

HOTELS

Belle Etoile (53.29.51.44). Charming old house facing the river. Perfect vine-shaded terrace for hot days. ROOMS B–E. MEALS C–F. Open early April–15 October.

Périgord, route de Vitrac, 4km SE (53.28.36.55). Rare 'three-chimney' Logis de France; garden, swimming-pool. Quiet. ROOMS E. MEALS C–F. Shut 14 February–early March; Sunday evening, Monday in winter.

RESTAURANT

Plume d'Oie (53.29.57.05). 'Absolutely charming and romantic atmosphere,' says *Le Bottin Gourmand*. Terrace above river. MEALS B–F. Open March–30 November. Shut Monday except evening midsummer.

ROUFFIGNAC
[Dordogne]

In a fit of pique because they were losing, and in revenge for the
success of the French Resistance, SS troops of *Das Reich* division
systematically burned down this old town north of Les Eyzies in
1944 – a singularly mindless act of vandalism, worthy of Julius
Caesar in his invasion of Gaul. The 1530 church alone survived.
It has some strangely profane decorations on its doorway of
sirens and other temptresses. The town has been rebuilt and is
the centre for visiting the extraordinary Grottes de Rouffignac,
5km S – dry caves rediscovered at least as early as the fifteenth
century with literally hundreds of engravings of horses, ibex,
rhinoceroses, bison and mammoths, plus a considerable amount
of more modern graffiti. The cave, open to the public, is 5km
long but you visit it by train (open Easter to November daily;
Sunday only rest of the year).

When the engravings were discovered in 1956, the experts
shouted, 'Fakes!' The same cry arose about most prehistoric cave
drawings but strangely there were many of these and it had
taken a suspiciously long time to find them. Now it is mainly
agreed that the majority of the drawings were made in the
Aurignacian and at the end of the Magdalenian period, around
40,000 years ago, but down the centuries enthusiasts added to
them as well as adding graffiti. The frieze of two stags locked in
combat is surely either remarkable or a quite recent fake.

Château l'Herm , 6km NW of Rouffignac, stands in almost
total isolation on a hilltop, its sightless windows looking out from
its empty shell. When Jean III de Calvimont built it in the heart
of the Barade Forest in 1512, it must have been an attractive,
proud manor. Jean was president of the Bordeaux *parlement* and
Louis XII's Ambassador to Rome. But his family seemed dam-
ned. His son, Jean IV, was murdered in L'Herm. His granddaughter, Marguerite, was killed on the orders of her husband,
François d'Aubusson, whether for her infidelity or because he
wanted to replace her with someone younger, I have never
discovered.

Last century Eugène Le Roy chose it as the manor of the
villainous nobleman who persecuted the peasants in his novel,

Jacquou le Croquant, published in 1899. The hero Jacquou burned down the château. And to visitors the legend of the novel has taken over the ruins of l'Herm. There are guided tours from 1 July to 31 August (shut Wednesday), but you can see it fairly clearly at any time.

SAILLAC
[Corrèze]

A hamlet on Dordogne–Corrèze border SW of Collonges-la-Rouge (*see* page 108) Saillac is known for its Romanesque church and remarkable carved doorway protected by a vestibule (called a 'narthex').

LE SAILLANT
[Corrèze]

Le Saillant is at the mouth of the Vézère Gorges in a lovely setting. A beautiful old bridge crosses the river and on the right bank you can see a twelfth-century manor house.

Le Saillant is not easy to find. From Brive, take the D901 NW, then right on the D148 passing near to Allassac. The road gets narrower as it runs by the river and reaches Le Saillant hamlet. Or drive into Allassac and take the slightly wider D134 left. This is lovely undulating scenery. There are few roads by the river through the wild country northwards but you can see the gorges from roads near Vigeois (*see* page 189), Uzerche (page 184) and Treignac (page 178). Or you can take a train from Allassac running almost alongside the river to Uzerche, where it bears left to Limoges – a lovely ride beside the gorges.

SAINTE-ALVÈRE
[DORDOGNE]

Charming little old town NW of Le Bugue on the river Louyre, in lovely country with fine views. Has ruins of a twelfth-century castle, including a gateway with truncated tower and two other towers. It was burned down after the Revolution by the dreaded Joseph Lakanal, sent by Paris to rule Dordogne.

MARKET Monday

ST ARMAND-DE-COLY
[DORDOGNE]

This tiny village, a hide-out in a small valley E of Montignac, once had an abbey housing 200 Augustinian canons. Only the abbey ramparts and a huge fortified church remain. It is indeed a formidable church, giving us some idea of the fear and turbulence of the Middle Ages, when churches were not just places of worship but also the only refuge from armed bands, who called themselves soldiers, and roamed France looting, raping and killing. The belltower of the church seems to have nothing to do with religion. It is a fortress tower, without windows – just a few holes for firing through. Monks and villagers could climb to successive levels to defend themselves, withdrawing climbing beams behind them. Hidden staircases and hollow pillars add to the defences. The beautifully proportioned nave under its domed roof has a gallery with a series of doors so that villagers could run round firing down on attackers. The altar is lit by just three narrow windows with one round open window above.

In a scenic valley W of the D704 Sarlat–Montignac road, 4km W of St Amand, is Château de la Grand-Filolie, another piece of defensive architecture needed in the Hundred Years War. It is a manor house which is half castle and half farm, where the lord and his peasants all tried to find safety. It has a fifteenth-century mansion with a windowless wall, a Renaissance manor, a polygon defence tower, various square towers with defence slits, and at the main entrance you can still see the supports for a drawbridge.

ST ANDRÉ-D'ALLAS
[Dordogne]

Near Sarlat just off the D25 westward, also signposted from the
D47 Les Eyzies road. The bishops of Sarlat used to have houses
here and it was called Allas l'Évêque. The Romanesque church
roofed in stone was their chapel. A plaque in a corner of the
churchyard is a memorial to a Resistance fighter, Emmanuel
Perera, executed there on 26 June 1944, 'mort pour la France'.
The other church of St André was rebuilt after the Religious
Wars.

Château du Roc is a splendid Louis XV building in golden
stone flanked by two wings and many dormer windows in its
roof. It stands proudly on a rock with a stone terrace.

Just N at Breuil-de-Bousseyrial are *cabanes*, small stone huts
which I was told pre-dated Roman Gaul. Their state of pre-
sentation amazed me. Then I was told locally later that they had
been 'restored' for a film in the late 1960s. Perhaps Asterix
passed this way!

ST ASTIER
[Dordogne]

Although cement works down by the river Isle do not improve
the beauty of this ambitious little town W of Périgueux, it has its
holiday visitors who come to shop from their campsites and *gîtes*
or to seek the excellent fishing. Its Renaissance houses and old
mansions are worth seeing. So, too, is the fourteenth-century
church, much repaired as a result of war damage over centuries
but still keeping a most impressive belltower, heavily buttressed
and decorated with blind arcades.

Among several local châteaux, the best is Puy-Ferrat to the
E, with two huge circular towers, built in the fifteenth and
sixteenth centuries.

St Astier suffered from wars. Its original abbey church was
destroyed by the Norsemen in the ninth century. The present
church, founded in 1013, was fortified by monks in the

thirteenth century. In the Hundred Years War, the English besieged and took the town, holding it from 1339–51. In the sixteenth century, town and church suffered in the Religious Wars. The Protestants took it, but it was so strong that it took six days of cannon-bombardment before they were successful. Then the armies of the Fronde, rebellious noblemen, pillaged it in 1652. The patient monks went on repairing and improving it until the Revolution.

St Astier is on the edge of the Double Forest and apart from a good weekly market there is a big autumn fair for poultry, *foie gras* and truffles, and farmers and merchants sell from under coloured umbrellas in the square.

MARKET Thursday

ST AVIT-SÉNIEUR
[DORDOGNE]

When Augustinian canons built themselves a church, they made a real job of it. In this very pleasant medieval village on the D25 between Beaumont and Cadouin they built a massive church fortified in the fourteenth century with a doorway fit for a castle and colossal towers on either side, linked by a watch-path. They were obviously expecting visitors. Some of the church is older, including the vaulting inside, put there after Albigensians had destroyed the church domes. Other bits and pieces from the abbey remain. But it is the village itself which attracts me – simple but friendly. St Avitus was a Roman soldier turned hermit. I sometimes wonder cynically if the Roman soldiers who opted for that life style were not deserters on the run! But he was taken prisoner by the Visigoths and 'converted' by them.

ST CYPRIEN
[DORDOGNE]

This village, built in terraces up the side of a hill, with pretty roads leading to Le Bugue and to Les Eyzies, is within 3km of the Dordogne river at the beginning of a very attractive stretch past Beynac (*see* page 84) and La Roque-Gageac (page 154) to Souillac. An interesting stretch, too, past bastides and castles with fascinating histories.

In a setting of hills and woods, St Cyprien's old houses cluster round yet another of these huge churches of an old Augustinian abbey, which still has its fortress-like belfry intact. The sixteenth-century abbey buildings are now used by the State Tobacco Board (*Régie des Tabacs*). Behind the town by the D48 and a side-street is the beautiful Renaissance Château de Fages, which has been much restored inside recently by an architect owner, including its painted walls and gilded ceilings. It has a small chapel with an ornate Renaissance porch.

MARKET Sunday

HOTELS

Abbaye (53.29.20.48). Good, comfortable, pricey. Swimming-pool. Nineteenth-century house. ROOMS E–G. MEALS D–G. Open 15 April–15 October.

Terrasse (53.29.21.69). Above-average Logis. ROOMS C–E. MEALS B–F. Open 1 March–1 November. Shut Sunday evening, Monday low season.

ST ESTÈPHE, ÉTANG DE
[*See* Nontron, page 147]

ST JEAN-DE-CÔLE
[DORDOGNE]

A beautiful village among lovely scenery on the D787 7km W of
Thiviers. Its charming houses are typically Perigordian, with
pretty roofs. A Gothic humpback bridge crosses the river Côle
and there is an old mill. The twelfth-century priory church in
yellow stone is not particularly pretty from outside. It once had a
huge dome but it kept falling down. It was 12 metres (over 39
feet) in diameter and last fell down in 1860. Now the apse is
roofed with wood. An unusual-shaped belfry is liberally broken
up by windows. A covered market is built into the church. The
two-sided eighteenth-century cloister which impressed me on
earlier visits is now privately owned and you can see it only from
across the bridge.

At the end of the wide street lined with yellow stone houses
is a *fontaine de l'amour*. If a girl drops in a pin and it falls on its
point, she is promised a wedding the following year. Three tiny

St Jean-de-Côle

houses have been made into a museum of crafts and life of the past.

The Château de la Marthonie is in the middle of the village. All but its two fourteenth-century towers was burned down in the Hundred Years War. It was rebuilt by the Marthonie family of Château de Puyguilhem (*see* Villars, page 191) in the fifteenth and sixteenth centuries. The arcaded gallery and ornamental staircase were added in the seventeenth century (open for guided tours 1 July to 31 August).

ST JULIEN-DE-CREMPSE
[DORDOGNE]

Despite its restored Romanesque church, St Julien-de-Crempse has nothing to tempt you to turn off the N21 on your way from Périgueux to Bergerac, except for its excellent hotel, Manoir le Grand Vignoble, and that sends many enthusiasts for food and horses hurrying the 12km from Bergerac. It is in a beautiful Louis XIV manor house in a park, and was built on the ruins of an English bastide. Its stables have sixty horses and ponies for riding and in its huge park are deer, bison, llamas, yak, cows, donkeys and camels.

HOTEL
Manoir le Grand Vignoble (53.24.23.18). See text. Swimming-pool, tennis, children welcome. Blend of regional, classic and modern dishes. ROOMS E–G. MEALS D–G. Restaurant shut 15 November–15 March.

ST LÉON-SUR-VÉZÈRE
[DORDOGNE]

In a beautiful stretch of scenery where the Vézère river loops round peaks 10km SW of Montignac. The greenery is so lush that it half-hides the villages, but from Côte de Jor, a 225-metre-high peak above it, are magnificent views of the river and the countryside bordered with oaks, pines and lovely chestnuts. It is a delightful village, quite an important port when goods were still carried by boat down the Vézère river.

It was a natural place to build châteaux for trade, defence and pleasant living. Several are still there.

Château de Clérans is in the village. It was built in the sixteenth century and is a graceful manor house, with battlemented turrets and corner towers. It has been well restored.

Château de la Salle, standing in the square, has a massive stone battlemented tower from the fourteenth century.

Château des Chabans is 3km W towards the Moustier river, which joins the Vézère 5km downstream from St Léon. Chabans is approached through a fine avenue of great cypresses. It was built in the sixteenth and seventeenth centuries and has two buildings at right angles, one flanked by a polygon tower, the other with a fine Louis XIII-style doorway.

The lovely Romanesque village church, reached through narrow streets, is among poplars and willows on a spur into the river. It flooded in 1961 and has been repaired. Its elegant belltower reflected in the water adds to its charm. Inside are traces of twelfth-century frescos, and the large windows are believed to date back to the eleventh century.

ST MICHEL-DE-MONTAIGNE
[DORDOGNE]

Michel Eyquem de Montaigne was born in 1533 in Château de Montaigne at St Michel-de-Montaigne, which is just N of the D936 at the western end of Dordogne. The only part of the home of the great philosopher which still exists is the library tower where he wrote. The rest was destroyed by a fire in 1884 and replaced by the present pseudo-Gothic building. On the beams of the tower are written texts in Latin and Greek. It is assumed that he wrote them but I have been told by French scholars that they were written by his father for his education.

Montaigne was born and lived in the château, and died there

in 1592. His great-grandfather, a Bordeaux wine merchant called Ramon Eyquem, bought the château to buy his family into the aristocracy. Montaigne had an extraordinary upbringing. His father employed a tutor to teach him Latin until he was six, and at home he was not allowed to speak French – only Latin – even to the servants. Then he was sent to the College of Guyenne to be taught by the Scottish humanist George Buchanan – in French.

From the age of twenty-one he practised law in Bordeaux. At thirty-five his father died, leaving him the Montaigne estate, where he lived like a country gentleman, made wine and wrote and published his books. He called his first book of comments on life and literature *Essaies*, meaning attempts or experiments. Thus was born the literary form we call 'Essays'.

He became Mayor of Bordeaux during terrible times of pestilence and of Religious Wars. A Catholic, he was a friend of Henri of Navarre, the Protestant leader, who stayed with him at his château. A constant advocate of tolerance, he pointed out that no two men ever had the same opinion on everything, and he tried to get the Protestants and the extreme Catholic Leaguers together, so winning the wrath of both.

He was a fearless original thinker and preached a philosophy contradicting all modern theories of competition and ruthless success-seeking. The true aim of life, he wrote, is not to win or to write books or to gain battles or lands and property but to live an ordered and tranquil life.

He wrote humorously, too. He had strong views on smells. He disliked the smell of Paris and loved the smell of good food. A true man of Périgord. The château is in the heart of Montravel vineyards.

ST PIERRE-DE-CÔLE
[DORDOGNE]

A very pretty village on the Côle river with water-mills and rapids by an old bridge. It is in lovely countryside, 7km W of Thiviers by the pretty D78, which continues to Brantôme.

The river swings round the ruins of Château du Bruzac, whose lord ruled the lands all the way to Limoges in the Middle Ages. Du Guesclin took Bruzac in 1371 and the original château was demolished in 1387. A Renaissance château was built on its ruins and of this seven towers, round and octagonal, now remain. From the old château a ruined chapel called *des Ladres* remains and you can see the holes through which lepers received the sacraments because they were not allowed into church.

ST ROBERT
[CORRÈZE]

Although it is just over the Corrèze border near Ayen, St Robert is surrounded by typical Perigordian scenery of hills planted with poplars and walnuts. There is a good view of the country-side from the terrace of the town hall (*mairie*). The church is partly from the twelfth century and was fortified in the four-teenth century.

HOTEL
Mont Bel Air (55.25.12.82). Simple, cheap, comfortable Logis. ROOMS B–C. MEALS A–D. Shut February; Wednesday.

SALIGNAC-EYVIGUES
[DORDOGNE]

A charming little town of narrow streets and lovely houses on the D60, which joins the N89 at Larche to D704, 9km N of Sarlat. It is known for its great medieval château of the twelfth century, surrounded by ramparts. It was built by the Salignac family, of which Fénelon, the writer, was a member (*see* Château de Fénelon, page 118). They bought it back after the Revolution and apparently they still own it.

The vast château is called *rude* by the French, which is like the old English word meaning unrefined or a bit crude, but it is certainly formidable. The central building with mullioned windows is flanked by two round towers with dunce's caps and a great square tower at the other end. At the top of a fine Renaissance staircase are rooms with Louis XIII and Louis XIV furniture. The family added a chapel in the thirteenth century. (Open in season, except Tuesday; Sunday afternoon.)

There is still a covered market in the village square.

MARKETS Second Thursday and last Friday of each month

HOTEL

Terrasse, place de la Poste (53.28.80.38). ROOMS C–E. MEALS A–E. Open early April–15 October.

SARLAT
[*See* Major Towns, page 50]

SAUSSIGNAC
[DORDOGNE]

This village on the D4, a lovely little road SW of Bergerac in the SW corner of Dordogne, was a town of great importance and a centre of justice in the Middle Ages and later. In 1286, Marguerite Budel, Countess of Bergerac and Viscountess of Turenne, gave Saussignac '*avec tous droits de haute, moyenne et basse justice*' (all rights of administering high, middle and low justice) to the noble family d'Estissac, who had a château there.

In the sixteenth century, the beautiful and charming Louise de la Beraudière, wife of Louis d'Estissac, lived there. She was a famous and popular hostess. Brantôme paid court to her. She captivated Rabelais, who had been her husband's tutor, and Montaigne, who became a very close friend and devoted one of his essays to praising her.

The ruins of the Estissac family's *Tour de Lengève* are still in the village. Under its walls two great soldiers, the Earl of Derby and Du Guesclin, fought in the Hundred Years War.

The great Caumont-Lauzun family took over Saussignac in the Hundred Years War and in the early seventeenth century one of them started to build the enormous château that you can see now. The man who started it was the father of the Duke of Lauzun, whose intrigues, adventures and *affaires* caused a lot of trouble to Louis XIV. He was imprisoned for daring to seduce Louis' niece, Mademoiselle de Montpensier, known as La Grande Mademoiselle. She wanted to marry him. The King forbade her.

Meanwhile, in the seventeenth century, the castle had passed to Capitaine de Boisse, one of Louis XIII's great soldiers, who continued building it but was assassinated before he had quite finished. It remains unfinished but very impressive, with a great pavilion that is flanked by two large wings topped by a Monsart roof with dormer windows, and with great bay windows in the façades.

Saussignac is a jolly wine village, surrounded by vineyards, and is known especially for its sweet white wine Saussignac Moelleux – rich, strong and, unfortunately, rare. It is produced by the great expert from the Institute of Bordeaux and maker of wonderful Bergerac wines, Pierre-Jean Sardoux, in the next village, Razac-de-Saussignac at his Château Court-les-Mûts (*see* Wine, page 23). You can taste it there – and they speak English. Or you can try the same wines with the excellent food of the brilliant young chef Dèscard Thierry at the Hôtel à Saussignac, the friendly centre and meeting place of the village.

2km down a side-street is Gageac-et-Rouillac, a hamlet of delightful houses, and a fourteenth-century fortress-castle with corner towers, Château de Gageac, owned by Geoffroy de Vivans, the Protestant commander in the Religious Wars.

HOTEL

Saussignac (53.27.92.08). See text. Outstanding cooking and value for money. ROOMS C–D. MEALS C–D. Shut part February; Sunday evening, Monday evening in winter.

SAVIGNAC-LEDRIER
[Dordogne]

For three centuries Périgord was known for its iron foundries producing arms, especially cannons, but the producers did not keep up with improved techniques and there were few left by this century. One of the last was Savignac-Ledrier, which closed in 1930. It is attached to the château, called la Forge – a fine manor in a picturesque setting. The main building is medieval, flanked by round towers. It was restored in the Renaissance. A lovely gate in the park is decorated with Moorish designs.

The village is SE of Lanouille on the Auvézère river in very attractive countryside.

SÉGUR-LE-CHÂTEAU
[Corrèze]

The old houses of this ancient market village 9km NW of Pompadour are reflected in the waters of the Auvézère river beneath the great ruins of the castle. This was the native village of the original Counts of Limoges, who were ancestors of Henri IV, so a house built with timbered walls and mullioned windows is known as 'The House of Henri IV'. Quite a lot are called this in France: he was the most popular king. From the watch-path of the castle there are good views of the old houses with brown roofs, of the river looping round the hillock on which the castle stands, and of the valley beyond.

SERGEAC
[Dordogne]

Opposite St Léon (*see* page 163) on the Vézère river, this hamlet is yet another of those very pleasant villages where, if you find a *gîte*, you can spend a delightful holiday exploring the countryside. It is on the D65, between Montignac and Les Eyzies, and is a market village. It has ruins of an ancient *relais* of the Knights Templars, a thirteenth-century manor ringed by old stone-roofed houses. A tower is bedded into a farmhouse. The church is fortified.

In the cliffs are fine prehistoric caves, and 500 metres down-river is the little museum of prehistory at Castel-Merle (*see* Les Eyzies Caves, page 59).

RESTAURANT

Auberge de Castel-Merle (53.50.70.08). Called the Belvedere when I first found it. Combines a good view with good classical Peri-gordian cooking. Good value. MEALS A–C. Open 1 April–31 October. Shut Monday except midsummer.

SERVIÈRES-LE-CHÂTEAU
[CORRÈZE]

Overlooks a gorge in the river Glane very close to the Gorges de la Dordogne and the Chastang dam and lake. It is surrounded by jagged rocks and great pines.

The big castle once belonged to the Viscount of Turenne. In the First World War, captured German officers were imprisoned in it. They set light to it. It has been rebuilt and when I last passed it was a nursing home.

The beautiful D29 winds down to the Dordogne river and the Chastang Dam. A balcony on the way, reached on foot, gives a splendid view over the dam and lake.

SIORAC-EN-PÉRIGORD
[DORDOGNE]

At the meeting of several roads to interesting places and on the Dordogne river between Beynac and Limeuil, Siorac has become quite an important little tourist centre in this age of *gîtes*. Once it dominated river-traffic from its castles, the last of which was built in the seventeenth century and now houses the town hall in one wing. Holiday-makers come into the village to shop, especially at the Wednesday market, and for the swimming, boating and fishing here. A good place to stay for exploring the Dordogne and Cadouin, Belvès, Les Eyzies and Sarlat.

MARKET Wednesday

HOTELS

Scholly, place Poste (53.31.60.02). I have known it for many years. Once famous for classic French cooking, it has bowed a little to modern, but regional and classic dishes are still on the menus. Away from traffic; shady terrace and peace. Good wine cellar. ROOMS C–F. MEALS E–G. Open all year.

Auberge Petite Reine, 1km S on D710 (53.31.60.42). Good holiday or weekend hotel with well-equipped rooms in pavilions around two swimming-pools. In July and August a club operates providing some entertainment. ROOMS D–E. MEALS B–E. Open 15 April–15 October.

Escale, le Port (53.31.60.23). 'Three-chimney' Logis, recommended to me for value. ROOMS A–B. MEALS A–E. Open Easter–1 November.

SORGES
[DORDOGNE]

A French tourist guide to Périgord I have at home dismisses Sorges as 'a little commune on the Route Nationale Périgueux–Thiviers. Some hotel-restaurants. *Tous commerces.*' But that was published in 1981. In April 1982 Sorges opened La Maison de la Truffe (the House of Truffles), and that has made it a village of pilgrimage for gourmets and gourmands as well as honest gluttons like me.

The museum is in the Syndicat d'Initiative and is interesting and erudite rather than exciting – a history of truffles, how and where they grow, press-button film on how they grow beneath oak trees under the earth and are hunted with pigs and dogs. There is a section on truffle cuisine, the history of the truffle, and, of course, the truffle and Venus – for the truffle is an aphrodisiac to true believers. It certainly was to Madame de Pompadour. There are also one-hour walks to show you where and how truffles grow, and a shop where you can buy them – fresh or tinned. They are very expensive – but what a splendid souvenir of Périgord to slice thinly into an omelette. (Museum open afternoons except Tuesday; mornings also in July, August.)

Sorges is a good market centre, especially for truffles, of course. In August it holds a famous Dog Show and Fair, where dogs are judged, bought and sold. I wonder if you could buy a genuine, trained truffle hound?

The village is on the N21. Its church has a domed roof and massive square belfry. The thirteenth-century Château de Jaillac was truly built for defence, for it has almost blind walls except for seventy-five loopholes for firing arrows. Inside there are fine chimneys and a stone staircase. Its huge rooms are furnished with pieces from various centuries.

Sorges also has two holiday villages and a programme of entertainment in summer.

TOURIST INFORMATION Syndicat d'Initiative
(53.05.90.11)
MARKET Friday

HOTELS

Mairie, facing church (53.05.02.11). Old-style village hotel of comfort. Terrace faces village square, the back faces countryside. Locals go there for true Perigordian cuisine of Jacqueline Leymarie. ROOMS B–D. MEALS B–G. Shut 18–24 June; 22–31 October; 3–18 January; Wednesday.

Auberge de la Truffe, on N21 (53.05.02.05). Very pleasant inn with garden for summer eating. Modern bedrooms. Outstanding Perigordian dishes (stuffed goose neck; *poule au pot*). Jacqueline has a hand in it! Visits on weekends to truffle trails and goose farms. ROOMS C–D. MEALS A–F. Shut 24 June–4 July; 15–22 October; 16–29 January; Monday.

TERRASSON-LA-VILLEDIEU
[Dordogne]

I have always loved this small market town astride the Vézère. The busy N89 from Périgueux to Brive passes just above it but few of the hurrying, worrying drivers seem to notice what a delightful place it is. Come to it on the little 'white' road from Condat, through the valley with wooded slopes alongside the Vézère, or by the very attractive D63 from the south. It is wonderful on Thursday, the main market day, especially in autumn when the chestnuts come in from the groves, which you can see beside the little roads to the south, or later when the truffles come in.

The old town is on one side of the river, the newer town on the other side, joined by a modern bridge and a twelfth-century medieval bridge. The old town rises up the hillside in terraces from a twelfth-century port to the fifteenth-century church. From the church terrace you can see right over the slate roofs of the houses which run in seeming disorder down to the river, to the wooded countryside beyond. The ramparts of a ruined château have been terraced. The river is lined with poplars and walnut plantations.

MARKETS Daily (main market on Thursday)

HOTEL
Willer, 6 rue Jean-Jaurès (53.50.06.93). Simple rooms. Good-value meals. ROOMS A–B. MEALS A–D. Shut 14 February–1 March; Sunday in winter.

THÉNAC
[Dordogne]

The first shots in the Hundred Years War were fired from a now destroyed castle near Thénac, a village SW of Bergerac which was then on the edge of French-held territory and Gascony, which had come under the English Crown since Henry Plantagenet had married Eleanor of Aquitaine (*see* History and

Art, page 29). Thénac is still on the borders of Dordogne and Gironde.

Philip VI of France wanted Gascony, and did all he could to prevent trade between Gascon Bordeaux and England. In 1337 he used an incident with the Gascons to declare Gascony confiscated from the English crown, and sent an army into the Dordogne–Gironde valley. The first cannon shot was fired from the Château de Puyguilhem, in the village of that name 3km S of Thénac. Don't confuse it with the Château de Puyguilhem near Villars (*see* page 191). This one has gone, but Château de Panisseau, which the English ruled, 3km N of Beynac on the river Bessage, is still there and put to very good use. In 1363, the Seigneur de Panisseau paid homage for his title to the Prince of Wales – the Black Prince. Now you can visit this delightful thirteenth-century château to taste the wine – two whites (one of Sauvignon, one made of half Sauvignon and half Sémillon grapes) and a red with long-lasting flavour which has twice won a gold medal at the great Mâcon Wine Fair.

THÉNON
[DORDOGNE]

A busy little town lying just below the N89 Périgueux–Brive road where it meets the D67 to Montignac, which has a really genuine old-style market on Tuesdays, not a show-market for tourists. It is a splendid place to buy fresh local food. Just outside is a pleasant small lake where you can take out a rowing-boat, swim or get a snack lunch with wine from a hut-café.

In the Middle Ages it was a fortress town – almost a military camp around a château owned by the Hautefort family. The English burned it down.

MARKET Tuesday

THIVIERS
[DORDOGNE]

The busy N21 skirts this very pleasant small town 37km NE of Périgeux, and you can walk round it in reasonable peace to explore its old houses, its lovely church, its Château de Vaucocour, and its attractive park. It is a busy agricultural centre and has many markets and fairs. The Saturday market lures people from far around, even from Brantôme, and its fairs for *foie gras*, truffles, poultry, *confits* and terrines, from November to February, are famous. Try the local goat's milk cheese called Thiviers with a glass of Monbazillac wine. There are plenty of restaurants in town.

The church, built from the twelfth century onwards, with a belltower added in the nineteenth century, has, inside, some extraordinary Romanesque sculptures designed to frighten medieval church-goers into behaving themselves. A large bird attacks a man plucking grapes and monsters swallow people, who cling fearfully to branches. Men try to get away by riding on monsters' backs or fleeing on foot. Samson is busy defeating a lion and Jesus hands the keys of heaven to St Peter while Mary Magdalen stands by carrying her jar of oil, with which she has anointed Jesus' head.

The château, with towers and turrets looking down on the Isle valley, was built in the sixteenth and seventeenth centuries, but has been much restored.

TOURIST INFORMATION place Maréchal-Foch (high
season – 53.55.12.50)
MARKET Saturday
FAIRS November – February (see text)

HOTELS

France et Russie, 51 rue Gén-Lamy (53.55.17.80). Comfortable, but no restaurant. ROOMS C–E.

St Roch, 2 ave de Gaulle (53.55.00.11). Auberge in old house, good cheap menus and reasonable carte prices. Five rooms. ROOMS C–D. MEALS A–E. Shut February; Tuesday.

THONAC
[Dordogne]

A very welcoming town on the D706, 6km S of Montignac and on the Vézère river. The riverside Château de Losse is a delight – quite one of the most attractive in Dordogne, both inside and out. It is open, alas, only from 1 July to 15 September, but that is not surprising because it is still a residence. Renaissance in style, it was built in the sixteenth century by Jean de Losse, Governor of Périgord, on the remains of his thirteenth-century castle, which was partly destroyed by Protestants. It stands on a rock above the river with dry moats protecting the other sides. A super balustraded terrace overlooking the river is supported by a big bowed arch which, given glass windows and doors, would make a magnificent sun-lounge. The two main buildings meet at a round tower and from the land-side the two buildings form a court with right-angled defence walls, which have corner turrets and a fortified gate.

I would love to live in Château de Losse! The sixteenth- to seventeenth-century furniture is beautiful, the tapestries superb. The original Flemish tapestries have kept their colour so well that you could believe them to be reproductions. The Florentine tapestry in the main chamber, 'Return of the Courtesan', is delightful.

At Le Thot, 2km N of Thonac, is a most interesting centre of prehistoric art, showing paintings, films and a tableau of cave paintings in the setting of the time when they were made.

In the park here you can see walking around some of the animals which our ancestors painted – bison, wild boar, deer, stags, tarpan horses.

HOTELS

Archambeau, place Église (53.50.73.78). Friendly inn run by the same family for years. Perigordian cooking. Sensible prices. Rooms C–D. Meals A–D. Shut 13 November–13 December.
Îles (53.50.70.20). Superior holiday Logis de France with swimming-pool. Very good cooking. Rooms D–E. Meals C–G. Open 1 April–26 November.

TOURTOIRAC
[DORDOGNE]

A happy, small market town on the Auvézère river 7km W of Hautefort, it sleeps in winter, except on market day, but livens up in summer when a few holiday-makers pass this way. It is known to scholars for its sparse ruins of an eleventh-century Benedictine abbey, but to me for the absurdly heroic adventures last century of a man whose tomb is in the cemetery – Orélie-Antoine I, King of Aurucania.

Antoine-Orélie du Tounens was born in Périgord in 1825. By 1858 he was a little-known lawyer in Périgueux, set for a life of dull comfort and anonymity. Something, however, fired his imagination and roused him from the half-dead. From somewhere he must have heard or read strange tales of South America. He became enthused by a scheme to bring him adventure, wealth, position and fame.

Auvezère River

He borrowed a lot of money and sailed for Chile. On the borders of Chile and Argentina he was greeted by the Indians as a liberator, gathered an army and in 1860 proclaimed himself King of Aurucania.

The Chilean Government was not pleased. They sent out a force to capture him, and deported him to France. So he borrowed more money and set out for Patagonia in Argentina, landing there secretly in 1869. He went through unbelievable adventures before being deported again. He made two more attempts before retiring to Tourtoirac. Presumably he could get no more backers, so France had to do without its South American kingdom. He died in Tourtoirac in 1878.

There is good fishing around Tourtoirac.

MARKET Third Tuesday of each month

HOTEL

Voyageurs (53.51.12.29). Shaded quiet garden by the river. Readers of my *Complete Travellers' France* have praised Mme Levignac's Perigordian cooking for years. Splendid value. ROOMS B–D. MEALS A–C. Open all year.

TREIGNAC
[CORRÈZE]

Delightful-looking town rising in tiers above the Vézère on D940, N of the Monédières Massif. Upstream the river is dammed to make a lake and flows fast through boulders past Treignac. You can get a gorgeous view of the town from the attractive D16 NW. The scenery around is superb. There is a Gothic bridge over the river from which you can see the old houses with slate roofs and the ruins of the castle looking down. In the higher town there are groups of old houses with turrets and carved doorways, and a granite fifteenth-century covered market.

Rocher des Folles, of huge granite rocks, lies SW of the town by a signposted road and a walk of about twenty to twenty-five minutes up a hill and down a narrow path through heather typical of this area. This is a fairly wild gorge. From the rocks you can see several Vézère gorges.

A dam and lake can be found 4km N of Treignac.

MARKETS 6th and 22nd of each month

HOTEL

Lac, at the lake, 4km N on D940 (55.98.00.44). ROOMS A–D. MEALS A–C. Open 15 April–15 October.

TRÉLISSAC
[DORDOGNE]

East of Périgueux on N21, very near to the river Isle. Several châteaux are nearby. Best of them is Caussade, a very pretty little fifteenth-century fortress standing in a clearing in the Lanmary Forest. Each of the main façades has a square tower. The castle is not open to the public. Château de Septfonds was designed by the great Bordeaux architect Victor Louis, responsible for Bordeaux's famous theatre.

TRÉMOLAT
[DORDOGNE]

If you take the D703 E from Lalinde it swings away from the river just before you reach Mauzac. Instead, take the little D31 by the river from Sauveboeuf to Mauzac, the small port so important in the days of river transport but now almost sleeping. From here you can take one of the most spectacular and delightful drives in this part of France – over the Cingle de Trémolat. *Cingle* means 'meander', but here the Dordogne river sweeps in two enormous loops. The little road which climbs from Mauzac winds through woods above white cliffs, with superb views of the river below, lined with poplars. The best view is from the Belvédère de Racamadou. From a platform by the water-tower you can see the panorama of the river down to Limeuil and the countryside of fields and meadows to the Bergerac hills. But you may prefer to sit and relax on the terrace of the Panoramic Hotel, where the view is not quite so spectacular but the food and wine are good. The last stretch of road is the most attractive and leads to one of my favourite Dordogne villages.

Trémolat is not very pretty but it has a charming atmosphere and is very French – *so* French that Claude Chabrol chose it as a typical French village for his film *Le Boucher*. I am told that this was a sinister thriller and I suppose he chose a place so peaceful and pleasant to contrast and heighten the dastardly deeds.

Try to see Trémolat on a working day before the summer holidays, when officials and the mayor are wandering in and out of the vast old *mairie*, which looks like a big manor house, and the children are running out of the part of it which is used for a school to play on the terrace shaded with pollarded plane trees. Farm machines are being topped up with fuel at the friendly family-run garage which really looks like an old film set. Farmers and passing travelling salesmen slip into the family-run inn for a big, cheap, family-cooked lunch. Then the children run into the same inn to buy sweets on the way home from school, teenagers to have a coffee or a Coca-Cola and a look through the magazines on sale, and farmers and farm workers stop for a glass of wine or a *pastis* and a laugh. It is a true local inn, and warm and friendly, like the old village houses in the winding lanes around.

The only sinister and strange building is the church, built by the Benedictines in the twelfth century, which is like a fortress or prison from the outside and a huge old warehouse within. It was built, obviously, to double as a fortress, a defence against armed marauding bands and looting armies, and its 350 square-metre single nave could have held every person in the village. The belltower is a fortified keep. I have seen many fortified churches in France but none so obviously built for defence as this. It seems to have done its job, for no armies or robber-bands in the long and fearful medieval wars harmed it and even the Revolution left it unscathed. Time, weather and neglect did the only damage, and some of that has been restored. But it remains dark, damp and depressing.

The small Romanesque chapel of St Hilary in the cemetery has been beautifully restored and is used as the village church. It is brightened by five modern stained-glass windows by Paul Becker.

In contrast to the church, the village *logis*, Le Vieux Logis, is exquisite. Over years Madame Giraudel-Destord, and later her son Bernard Giraudel, turned it with loving care from a snug, village Logis de France with stables and a farm-garden into an absolutely delicious little Relais et Châteaux hotel – surely the best Logis in France and certainly one of my favourite country hotels in the world.

The stables have been converted into charming, comfortable bedrooms. In the main building the bedrooms are superbly decorated and furnished with antiques. The garden is lovely, the food is delicious, the welcome is warm. It is expensive and worth every franc. It is cool in hot summer sun, warm with log fires in winter.

HOTELS

Le Vieux Logis (53.22.80.06). See text. ROOMS G. MEALS F–G. Shut 15 November–15 December; 15 January–15 February. Restaurant shut Wednesday lunch; Tuesday in winter.
Panoramic, Cingle de Trémolat 2½km on D31 (53.22.80.42). Lovely views. See text. ROOMS C–E. MEALS B–F. Shut 2 January–2 March. Restaurant shut Monday in winter.

TULLE
[*See* Major Towns, page 56]

TURENNE
[CORRÈZE]

This picturesque cluster of turreted and towered houses of the fifteenth and sixteenth centuries around the grim ruins of its castle, 16km SE of Brive, was from feudal times until 1738 the seat of a powerful *vicomte*, independent of Kings of France, collecting its own taxes and minting its own money. To the peasants it was a little paradise compared with most of France, for they paid rents to one *vicomte*, not to grasping minor nobles, and they did not have to pay tithes to the church. These were sometimes so high that they brought whole farming communities very near to starvation and were one of the major causes of the Revolution.

The *vicomtes* ruled 1200 small towns and villages, could give noble titles, create offices and set up consulates. The greatest of the Turenne family were two men called Henri de la Tour d'Auvergne. The first was *vicomte* in the sixteenth century. He became a Protestant, was one of the most successful commanders and a friend of Henry IV. The second Henri de la Tour d'Auvergne, son of the first, was called the Great Turenne. He was a Protestant and a soldier, and after great successes in the field joined the Fronde, the rebellious nobles. After their defeat he retired to his estates. But he came out of retirement to join Mazarin, who had succeeded Richelieu as the power in France. He returned to the Royal Army, defeated the former Commander-in-Chief Condé, who led the rebels, took much of the Low Countries from the Spaniards, became a Catholic and was made Marshal-General (Commander-in-Chief) of France. He crossed the Rhine to invade the German States, ravaged whole areas of Germany, but was killed at Sasbach in 1675. Louis XIV thought so much of him that he was buried beside Du Guesclin at St Denis. His tomb is now in the church of Les Invalides in Paris. Napoleon considered him the finest soldier of modern times.

A later Vicomte de Turenne sold the rights of his ancestors to Louis XV in 1738 and Turenne came under Paris.

The great castle was ruined in the Revolution. Walking up a steep hill to it you pass the old houses. A stepped ramp leads past a solid rock wall to the old guardroom chamber, but only the outer defences and two towers remain. The rest has become a very attractive garden. At the far end is the Tour de César in which a spiral staircase leads to an open platform. The panoramic views from there are enormous, eastward to the mountains of the Massif Central on clear days. The church tower is at the very end of the castle rocks. (Castle is open daily 1 April to 30 September; Sunday afternoon rest of the year.)

The town is built almost entirely in white limestone, in contrast to Collonges-la-Rouge (*see* page 108) nearby in red sandstone.

RESTAURANT

Maison des Chanoines, route de Château (55.85.93.43). Sixteenth-century stone house where the cooking is good and regional. Book in season. MEALS C–E. Shut December, January; Tuesday evening, Wednesday except July, August.

TURSAC
[DORDOGNE]

6km NW from Les Eyzies on the D706, Tursac is across the river Vézère from La Madeleine cliff caves which were turned into a fortress (*see* Les Eyzies Caves, page 59). Tursac has a fortified mansion of the fifteenth to sixteenth centuries, Château de Marzac, with four round towers at the corner of its living quarters, and a Romanesque, domed fortified church.

USSEL
[CORRÈZE]

A pretty town, 631 metres above sea level in the foothills of Millevaches Plateau, on the N89, the road which runs all the way from Bordeaux through Périgueux and Brive to Clermont Ferrand in the Auvergne and on to the N7 near Lyon. Ussel is 21km N of Neuvic (*see* page 145).

It has many attractive houses with turrets in the old town, mostly in the side-streets around place Joffre. The coats of arms of the original owners are still above many of the doorways.

Behind the covered market is a fine and elegant Renaissance

mansion, Hôtel de Ventadour (*see* Neuvic, page 146), the comfortable house which the Dukes of Ventadour built in the sixteenth century, preferring it to the strong but uncomfortable fortress which they abandoned near Egletons.

The museum of traditional local arts and crafts is in two old buildings in different parts of the town – Hôtel du Juge Choriol, a renovated eighteenth-century mansion, and the old Chapelle des Pénitents (both open daily 1 July to 31 August; at other times apply at town hall; tel. 55.72.27.27).

Ussel is a good centre for exploring the virtually unknown countryside of Corrèze, a very green land of tree-covered hills, valleys with little rivers and tiny roads winding through to secret hamlets. It is an important railway junction for lines from the north joining east-west lines.

TOURIST INFORMATION place Voltaire (55.72.11.50)
MARKETS Wednesday, Saturday

HOTELS

Grand Hôtel Gare, Restaurant Châteaubriand, ave P. Sémard (55.72.25.98). Sophisticated classical cooking. ROOMS C–D. MEALS B–F. Shut 15 October–5 November; 10–28 February; Friday.
Midi, ave Thiers (55.72.17.99). Simple, cheap, good value. ROOMS B–C. MEALS A–C. Restaurant shut Sunday low season.
Gravades, at St Dézery 4km NE on N89 (55.72.21.53). Strangely modern but pleasant building surrounded by greenery. Very nice regional bourgeoise cuisine. ROOMS D–E. MEALS C–E. Restaurant shut 20 December–1 January; Friday evening, Saturday lunch low season.

UZERCHE
[CORRÈZE]

The river Vézère almost encircles the ancient and beautiful town of Uzerche and there are so many belltowers, turrets and pepper-pot roofs crowded on to its hillside that it would make a splendid backcloth for a film of medieval life. It is on the very busy N20, 35km N of Brive, but luckily the road keeps to a low level and leaves the old town on the rock reasonably peaceful so that you can walk round to explore it, which is a delightful experience.

First go from the bridge, Pont Turgot, along the D3, which goes uphill to the suburb of Ste Eulalie, then look back. From here you can see the river, the old houses climbing up the rock, the twelfth-century clock tower of the church of St Pierre at the top, and below, among the houses, the old Château Pontier.

If you enter the old town from the south, go through the only remaining gate in the fourteenth-century fortifications, Porte Bécharie, next to which is a building with a square tower called Château Bécharie. You reach place des Vignerons, the former fruit market, surrounded by old houses and the oldest church in the town, the chapel of Notre-Dame. Walk along rue St-Nicolas, which takes you to the St Pierre church in place de la Libération. It was built in the eleventh to thirteenth centuries. Its clock tower has square lower storeys and an octagonal top storey. Against the SW corner is a stolid round tower with arrow-slits built in the fourteenth century to guard against attacks by the English or marauding *routiers*, the freelance soldiers. The pillars inside are sturdy enough for a fortress, too. Outside, from the Lunade Esplanade, you can see Vézère valley scenery.

On your way back through Porte Bécharie look up to the wall on your right. The motto on the town's coat-of-arms is '*Non Polluta*' – 'never sullied'. Charles V called the town 'Uzerche the Virgin' because it was never once taken by an enemy – not even the Moors.

In 732, after their defeat at Poitiers by Charles Martel, the Moors, who had invaded France from Spain, attacked Uzerche, but it held out for seven years because of its solid walls and eighteen fortified towers. The Moors finally had to give up. Local legend tells the same corny story about the town's deliverance as you can hear about dozens of besieged towns around Europe. I heard it first at Carcassonne. Here it is: decimated by famine and almost out of food, the townspeople killed their last calf and with their last reserves of corn presented it to the Moorish commander. He was convinced they must be getting secret supplies of food. So the Moors cut their losses and left.

TOURIST INFORMATION place Lunade (April–
September – 55.73.15.71)
MARKET 20th of each month

HOTELS

Teyssier, rue Pont-Turgot (55.73.10.05). A good, traditional little hotel with a garden on the banks of the Vézère. Big range of menus. ROOMS B–E. MEALS C–G. Shut 1 January–1 March; 14–22 October; Wednesday except evenings July, August.

Ambroise, ave Paris (55.73.10.08). Simple, comfortable. ROOMS B–C. MEALS A–D. Shut November; Saturday, Sunday except July, August.

VARAIGNES
[DORDOGNE]

Just off the D75 NW from Nontron, on the road to Angoulême, this town is proud of its produce and cuisine, especially turkeys, various mushrooms, and meringues and macaroons. On the Sunday before 15 August the village organizes a feast called a *Marende* at 5 p.m. in the courtyard of its fifteenth-century castle. It is part of a big and popular fair. Another centuries-old fair is held on 11 November, attended by people from all over Dordogne, Charente and Limousin. It is called *Foire aux Dindons de la Saint-Martin*, but is not only for turkeys, but all the food of the Varaignes area.

The château, with a strong square tower and polygonal stone staircase tower, contains a small museum of local folk art.

In the ancient narrow streets you can see signs on the old houses left from long ago, such as '*Aubergiste, loge à pied et à cheval*' – lodgings for foot travellers and horse-riders. Two fountains, St Jean and Ste Marguerite, still attract pilgrims looking for relief from rheumatism.

VARETZ
[Corrèze]

10km NW of Brive on the D901, and on the important Brive rail line, the village of Varetz is known for Castel Novel, the old château where the writer Colette lived, which is now a delightful Relais et Châteaux hotel.

Castel Novel had belonged to the family of her second husband, Henri de Jouvenel des Ursins, since 1844. Henri was a politician, editor-in-chief of the newspaper *Le Matin* and a great success with women. He was a lion of Paris literary circles but women called him the Tiger. He was living with the Comtesse de Comminges who was called the Panther. They had a son.

Suddenly he left the Panther and married Colette, who had been a very successful writer but was broke and had gone on the stage after her disastrous marriage to 'Willy', another journalist and writer who had put his name to her early novels of *Claudine* and claimed authorship. She liked Castel Novel and Henri's family. But she went back to the stage until she was pregnant. She was forty when her daughter was born in 1913. Her daughter stayed at the château with a nurse during the First World War, while she became a war nurse, then a war correspondent.

In the late 1920s Henri Jouvenal became French Ambassador in Mussolini's Rome. In 1935 he died of a heart attack on Champs-Elysées. She had not seen him or Château Novel for twelve years. They had been divorced since 1925.

The château with pepper-pot turrets is of medieval origin but has been much altered. The English took it in 1372. In its vast park are fine old oak trees. It now has three dining-rooms – one in a Louis XIII room with a fine monumental fireplace, another in Colette's old library and the third in a covered terrace overlooking the park. A hundred new trees have been planted and the owner has put in a swimming-pool, tennis-courts, a golf course and a practice range.

HOTEL

Castel Novel (55.85.00.01). See text. Described by Champérard, the French gastronome, as 'a palace of good taste, where comfort, courtesy and gourmandise make for a perfect stay'. Certainly very good indeed and justifiably very expensive. ROOMS G. MEALS F–G. Open early May–15 October.

VERGT
[DORDOGNE]

Now the top strawberry market of France, Vergt calls itself *'Capital de la Fraise'*, and that has all happened since 1971. But it was always known for its market for chickens, ducks, geese and *foie gras*, and in season for nuts.

Dordogne produces more strawberries than any other department in France. Peak months are May and June but often there is a September crop and forced fruit is sold as early as March. In Vergt, strawberries are sold by the tonne in the Friday market.

Vergt is on the D8 S from Périgueux which becomes the D21 a few kilometres further S, continuing to Bergerac. This is a more pleasant route than the N21 between the two big towns. The D21 follows the little river Caudau for some way.

A writer born in Vergt in 1830, J. C. Fulbert Dumonteil, did much to tell the outer world about the truffle and other great food products of Périgord. He called it *'perle noir du Périgord'* (the black pearl of Périgord). To novelist George Sand it was the *'pomme féerique'* (the magical potato) but to Colette's vivid imagination it was *'diamant noir'* (the black diamond), and that is certainly nearer the truth these days in price. Vergt is also known for perch from the tiny rivers and an *étang* to the south. It has a good rugby team, UAV, too.

MARKET Friday (mainly strawberries in season – see text)

FAIRS Fridays after 4 August and third Sunday in September

VEYRIGNAC
[DORDOGNE]

Tiny, peaceful village on a charming stretch of the Dordogne
river, downstream from Château de Fénelon. It is on the pretty
D50, which follows the left bank from Souillac to Grolejac. Down
a drive on the riverbank is Château de Veyrignac. It was built as
a feudal château in the Middle Ages, was converted into a
monastery, then made into a house by the Marquis de Therme,
one of Louis XIV's Marshals. It was altered in the eighteenth
century, but set alight by the *Das Reich* SS Division in 1944. It has
been beautifully restored.

VIGEOIS
[CORRÈZE]

Downstream from Uzerche on the Vézère, Vigeois is at the
mouth of the great Gorges de Vézère and 16km E of Pompadour. It has a charming medieval bridge over the river and
yet another Romanesque church, recently restored. It is at the
junction of many small roads ideal for exploring this virtually
unknown countryside and is only 28km N of Brive.

HOTEL
Semailles, 2 route de Brive (55.98.93.69). A good local inn with
seven rooms, plenty of variety in the dishes and good range of
meal prices. ROOMS A–D. MEALS B–F. Shut December,
January; Sunday evening, Monday low season.

VILLAMBLARD
[DORDOGNE]

Important agricultural town 22km from Bergerac and 28km
from Périgueux on the opposite side of the N21 from Vergt.
The slate-roofed market-hall is imposing. Like Vergt it is a
centre for strawberries.

The Château Barrière, which is on the edge of the town, saw fighting in the Hundred Years War and the Wars of Religion, but was not damaged until it was burned down accidentally in quite recent times. Its considerable remains look quite venerable in this pleasant town, which is a good centre for walks in the Landais Forest.

MARKET Monday

VILLARS
[DORDOGNE]

Caves, a castle and a pretty village of typical Perigordian houses around a sixteenth-century church. The village is on the D3 NE of Brantôme. The caves, 4km NE off the D82, include the splendid Grotte de Cluzeau, known for the purity of its trans-

Château de Puyguilhem

lucent stalagmites and stalactites, which are quite exquisite. A winding corridor leads to the chambers. Some walls are decorated with drawings in manganese oxide, made about 30,000 years ago. They include a sorcerer and several bison (cave open 15 June to 15 September).

The elegant Château de Puyguilhem, just outside Villars, reminds most people of châteaux on the Loire and was built at the same time as many of them, the beginning of the sixteenth century.

When François I went campaigning in Italy, he made his mother, Louise de Savoie, Regent of France. Mondot de la Marthonie, first President of the Bordeaux and Paris *parlements*, became her Chief Minister, with a lot of power. In keeping with his importance he had on old château outside Villars rebuilt, using brilliant sculptors. He died (probably poisoned) before it was finished. His son took over. Its main pavilion has a massive circular tower at one end, and a tower housing the carved main staircase at the other. After the Second World War it was in such a bad state that it was likely to be abandoned, but the Beaux Arts department took it over and have restored it excellently, furnishing it from other State-owned châteaux (shut Tuesday and mid-December to 1 February).

The sparse remains of the Abbey of Boschaud in Villars are being restored.

HOTEL

Castel (53.54.88.64). Nice old house in a garden. Good, traditional cooking, excellent value. ROOMS B–E. MEALS A–D. Open all year.

VILLEFRANCHE-DE-LONCHAT
[DORDOGNE]

This Villefranche is only just in the Dordogne department. Way W of Bergerac, it is only 23km from St Émilion, and sits on the crest of a rock looking down on its vineyards and the Château de Gurson, once owned by Henry III of England, but now in ruins.

The castle lake is popular for swimming and fishing. Villefranche-de-Lonchat was built as an English bastide.

VILLEFRANCHE-DU-PÉRIGORD
[DORDOGNE]

One of the first bastides built in the 1260s for Henry III of England by Alphonse de Poitiers, who was the brother of Louis VII. It kept changing hands between English and French, Catholics and Protestants, and was frequently badly damaged and rebuilt. It still has its market-hall, raised on pillars, and old stone arcaded houses near the church. It also has its old measuring and weighing scales for grain, walnuts and chestnuts.

Villefranche is at the SW end of Dordogne, just N of Loubejac and 4km from the border of Lot. It was originally on the borders of French territory and English Aquitaine, so suffered from attacks and sieges for centuries. It is surrounded by wooded hills in the heart of chestnut country, and has Saturday markets for nuts in October, November and December. In summer a Maison de Châtaignier, Marrons et Champignons is open. *Châtaignes* and *marrons* are two of the three major types of chestnuts. The forest of pine, oak and chestnut, with its clear streams, spreads right across the Lot border towards Cahors.

MARKET Saturday

HOTELS
Commerce (53.29.90.11). Charming, honey-coloured stone building with outside arcade making a terrace for views across the countryside. Family run, bar used by locals. ROOMS C–E. MEALS A–G. Open 1 April–15 November.
Bruyères, route Cahors (53.29.97.97). Logis with swimming-pool. ROOMS C. MEALS A–F. Shut 15–31 March; 15–30 November; 15–31 January; 15–28 February; Monday in winter.

VITRAC
[DORDOGNE]

Between La Roque-Gageac and Château de Montfort on the right bank of the Dordogne river. It has a little river-resort on the D46 with good fishing and swimming, hotels and campsite. Off the D46 by a winding lane is the old town signposted as Vitrac-Bourg. This has a massive Romanesque church in its square and next to it a 'Renaissance' château built in the nineteenth century. There are many old castles round here, including Château de Mas Robert, set alight by the Protestants in the Wars of Religion, now restored. Montfort is 4km upriver, Roque-Gageac 3km downriver, Domme 4km over the river on the D46 and Sarlat 6km N. Vitrac is a nice place to stay.

HOTELS

Plaisance, Le Port (53.28.33.04). *Very* pleasant. Garden by the river, swimming-pool. Family-run. ROOMS C–E. MEALS A–F. Shut 20 November–1 February. Restaurant shut Wednesday off season.

Treille, Le Port (53.28.33.19). Very agreeable. Nice riverside shaded terrace. Only six rooms. Good bourgeoise regional cooking. ROOMS B–C. MEALS A–F. Shut January, February; Tuesday.

RESTAURANT

Sanglière, at Les Veyssières, 3km NE on lanes (53.28.33.51). Good family Perigordian cooking in a little country restaurant. MEALS B–E. Open early April–30 September. Shut Sunday evening, Monday except July, August.

See also *La Ferme*, at Caudon-de-Vitrac (page 104).

MAPS

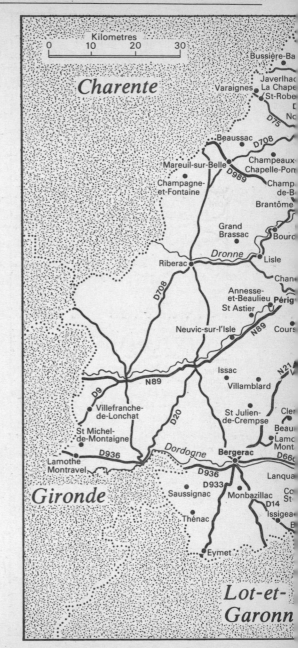

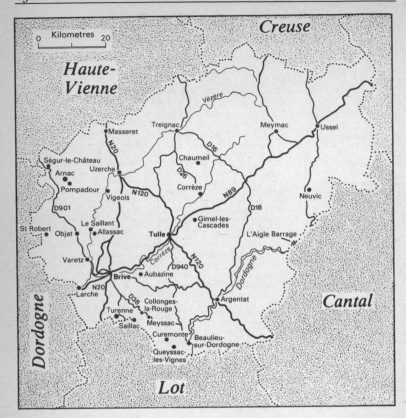

INDEX

Names of hotels and restaurants appear in *italics*.

All Pan books are available at your local bookshop or newsagent, or can be ordered direct from the publisher. Indicate the number of copies required and fill in the form below.

Send to: **CS Department, Pan Books Ltd., P.O. Box 40,**
                  Basingstoke, Hants.   RG21 2YT.

or phone: 0256 469551 (Ansaphone), quoting title, author
                 and Credit Card number.

Please enclose a remittance* to the value of the cover price plus: 60p for the first book plus 30p per copy for each additional book ordered to a maximum charge of £2.40 to cover postage and packing.

*Payment may be made in sterling by UK personal cheque, postal order, sterling draft or international money order, made payable to Pan Books Ltd.

Alternatively by Barclaycard/Access:

Card No.

Signature:

Applicable only in the UK and Republic of Ireland.

While every effort is made to keep prices low, it is sometimes necessary to increase prices at short notice. Pan Books reserve the right to show on covers and charge new retail prices which may differ from those advertised in the text or elsewhere.

NAME AND ADDRESS IN BLOCK LETTERS PLEASE:

Name

Address

3/87